Dr. Shannon;

I look forward to
your thoughts on
the weak attempt
to write a Book.

love,

Dr. Rob Bell.

P.s. See Acknowledgements ~

Mental Toughness Training for Golf

Start Strong Finish Strong

Dr. Rob Bell

authorHOUSE®

AuthorHouse™
1663 Liberty Drive
Bloomington, IN 47403
www.authorhouse.com
Phone: 1-800-839-8640

First published by AuthorHouse 4/27/2010

ISBN: 978-1-4490-6190-6 (e)
ISBN: 978-1-4490-6188-3 (sc)
ISBN: 978-1-4490-6189-0 (hc)

Library of Congress Control Number: 2010904265

Printed in the United States of America
Bloomington, Indiana

This book is printed on acid-free paper.

Acknowledgements

"Success has a thousand fathers, failure is an orphan."

I want to extremely thank all of the professional golfers who contributed to this book through your words and/or play: Jim Breech, Gary Christian, Garrett Clegg, Rickie Fowler, Jonathan Fricke, Scott Masters, Scott Moran, David Morland IV, Scott Stallings, Brendan Steele, Chip Sullivan, Peter Tomasulo, & Ron Whittaker.

To the Golf Professionals who helped make this possible: John Dal Corobbo, Perry Dotson, Don Essig III, Sam Froggatte, Colby Huffman, Brian Pierce, Jeff Schroeder, Blair Shadday, Barry Shular, Todd Smith, Jon Stutz, Scott Steger, & Darren Thomas.

I would like to especially thank all of the golf coaches who provided your time and guidance. Mike Fleck, Jamie Green, Mike Griffin, Mark Guhne, Derek Freeman, Sam Froggatte , Phil Parkin, Andrew Pratt, Bowen Sargent, Pat Sellers, Joe Skovron, Mike Small, & Randy Wylie.

To my many friends, mentors, and reviewers along the way: Frank & Sandy Bell, Camille Cassidy, Leslee Fisher, Noah Gentner, Rob Nahlik, Jason Grindstaff, Melinda Houston, Kerrie Kauer, Doug Moochio, Taryn Morgan, Tommy Pharr, Vanessa Shannon, Mitch & Mary Towe, Mark Tschaepe, Ash Patel, Joe Whitney, & Craig Wrisberg.

Thank you to the book cover artist, Daniel Hall, and the production team of Veronica Zan and Jennifer Slaybaugh.

My loving wife Nicole, and my incredible daughter Ryan, I can't express how much your love and support has helped. To Mom & Dad, thank you for bearing with me through the lost years. To my lord, a reverent nod and a wink of the eye.

Contents

The Bail Out Shot

"More careers have been ruined by searching rather than practicing."
—Colby Huffman

Not long ago, golfers tried to perfect playing the game of golf. Nowadays, golfers try to perfect the golf swing. This shift has resulted in a lack of mental toughness. The content within these pages is designed to introduce mental toughness training concepts and provide specific practices throughout. This book can be summarized in one sentence: *Make practice and play more difficult than actual competition.* When our practice is difficult, we can then learn our tendencies, our thoughts, our weaknesses, and our strengths. Each section is also littered with specific practices to reinforce mental toughness concepts. Only by preparing properly can we become mentally tough and maximize our potential.

Golf Is Difficult
*-Golfers are like tea bags, we don't know how
strong they are until in hot water.-*

Playing the illustrious Oakmont Country Club was definitely one of the joys of this young golfer's short playing career. Competing at Oakmont at age nineteen, with only six years of actual golf experience, was an incredible experience in itself. Oakmont is by far one of the toughest golf courses in the United States, annually ranked fifth in America's top courses, home to over eight U.S. Open championships. Even the "king," Arnold Palmer, failed to win a major tournament here on his home course. Few can walk on to this historic landmark outside of Pittsburgh and just play. You either have to be a guest of a member or play in an illustrious event like the U.S. Amateur. But when young Nick Flanagan walked onto Oakmont Country Club, he ended up becoming the first Australian in over a hundred years and the first foreign-born player in thirty-two years to win the U.S. Amateur. "I never played in any kind of atmosphere like that before," Flanagan said. "There were thousands of people out there. You're in a playoff for the most prestigious amateur tournament in the world. If I ever feel that much pressure again, I'll be very surprised" (U.S. Amateur). His U.S. Amateur win was even more remarkable, because he had only been playing for a short amount of time and because he had beaten an overwhelming favorite and "purebred golfer," Casey Wittenberg. As Cinderella stories are concerned, this definitely would have qualified, yet Nick Flanagan did not fade off into obscurity. Instead, he ascended to greatness. He proceeded to win three times during the 2006 season on the Nationwide Tour and was awarded a "battlefield" promotion onto the PGA tour.

The most interesting notion of this story is Nick Flanagan's rise to greatness in a relatively short amount of time. To date, there is only one other notable player to reach greatness in such a short amount of time, hall of famer Gary Player, who started playing at age fifteen. To illustrate this idea about the time it takes to reach heights of greatness, Krampe & Ericsson (1996) conducted research with expert musicians. They discovered that professional pianists all shared a similar characteristic. They all spent a certain amount of time within their passion. The authors found that the "best" performers spent approximately 10,000 hours of deliberate practice, the "good" players spent approximately 8,000 hours, and the amateurs practiced approximately 2,000 hours.[1] The sport of golf is no exception to this rule, because the time required for golfers to achieve "elite" or near elite status is ten years or 10,000 hours of intense involvement.

In the movie *Karate Kid*, Daniel Laruso (Ralph Machio) begins his training with Mr. Miyagi (Pat Morita) by finishing his seemingly endless yard work: "wax on, wax off," "sand the floor," "paint the fence," and "paint the house." It's only after Daniel revolts from all of the hard work that Mr. Miyagi finally reveals the method behind his training and Daniel puts together his arsenal of defense. Mr. Miyagi knew there was no shortcut other than the hours of repetition necessary to mimic and essentially overlearn the movements. Malcom Gladwell's best-seller *Outliers* translates the 10,000 hour rule into everyday examples by citing Bill Gates's never-ending hours of computer programming to the Beatles' constant nightly playing in clubs in England before they appeared on the Ed Sullivan show. Likewise, musicians such as Taylor Swift, John Mayer, and The Jackson Five became so successful because they practiced every day after school while their friends were playing.

UCLA head golf coach Derek Freeman often discussed the notion of 10,000 hours with his players. He won the NCAA championship in 2008 and orchestrated an undefeated 2008 fall campaign. He commented that the 10,000-hour conversation opened his players' eyes. In order to reach 10,000 hours, he juxtaposed what they currently did and what they had to do. He provided them the benefit of the doubt, assuming each of them effectively practiced two hours a day for five days a week, factoring in a combined two weeks off per year, equated to five hundred hours per year. Because these players are intelligent undergrads at a prestigious university, they ascertained quickly that they would have to work twice as hard as they currently did if they wanted to eventually turn professional.

Obviously, 10,000 hours of deliberate practice is a *lot of time,* but it is only required for the most elite. While most (of us) will not approach the elite level of play, we may have other goals of winning a collegiate tournament, club championship, amateur tournament, sectional tournament, or Friday afternoon money game. Because numerous hours of practice and play are required, there does not appear to be any shortcut to this process; however, one notion that is not addressed in the literature is why some players get more out of their practice than others.

The sport of golf is difficult. It involves many inherent aspects that are out of the golfer's control. For instance, control of the golf ball in flight is nearly impossible. Even the best mechanical devices designed for the sole purpose of driving or putting the golf ball cannot produce completely consistent golf shots. [2] Thus, it is practically impossible to land a shot in an exact location. Even professionals are faced with a high degree of failure and inconsistency.

No other sport has a target so disproportional to the field of play. Compared to the game of pool (small target/small playing field) or soccer (large target/large playing field); Golf requires the performer to "score" a very small target within an enormous playing field. For example, the field of play in golf can range from 6,600 to 7,400 yards, with each hole only four inches across.

Golf is also the only sport in which one cannot practice on the actual field before play begins. All other sports (e.g., basketball, soccer, football, baseball, and hockey) allow an orientation time to test the field of play. However, in golf, greens and fairways can firm up quickly, and wind directions can often change one's game plan or increase one's level of doubt. Uneven lies, divots, different cuts of rough, wind, direction, and in-between distances are all examples of variable factors within the actual course of play, but there are rarely—if ever—opportunities to practice with them.

Golf takes time. It has more "downtime" than any other sport. In the course of making seventy-two "shots," the average time per round of actual performance is approximately twelve minutes. As a result, there is an inordinate amount of time to think between shots, which unfortunately can be counterproductive to performance. If one adds the variable of slow play, it can affect the entire day on the course.

Perfection often occurs during practice. This paradox manifests itself on the range but is almost impossible to achieve during play. Again, think about the impossibility of hitting a shot to the exact location on the green. On the practice range, perfection or near perfection occurs often, because the range is a secure place devoid of pressure; however, expectations increase on the course because of that perfection achieved on the range. Golfers can groove the swing and execute perfect draws, fades, and more. If a shot is not executed properly, then another ball is quickly put into play until the desired outcome is achieved. These ephemeral episodes of perfection only add to the difficulty and frustration of actual play, because perfection on the course still remains impossible. What about the absurdity of an ace? A hole-in-one, one of the best shots that can occur, still counts one stroke against your score.

The harder one tries in golf, the worse one will usually do. This notion is repeated often throughout the game. When one tries to "muscle" a drive, it usually changes the technical soundness of the swing, resulting in a miss-hit. Pressure moments usually cause us to "try harder" which results in playing too tightly and "holding" onto the shot. Also, whenever we try to post a certain score and to "prove" ourselves, we usually play worse. Likewise, an accomplished player who is struggling with putting is usually just trying too hard to make it. The harder we try, the worse we usually do.

The numbers don't lie. One of the mental difficulties within the game is posting a bad score. Similar to standing atop a difficult ski slope, there is "no place to hide," and while the score does not lie, it does not tell the whole story. The posted score does not state that we played great except for one poor hole or that we really battled or that we were just in bad spots for most of the course. The increasing difficulty when we continually post poor scores is that we inherently know it does not reflect our *true performance.* As a result of spending a great deal of time within golf, part of our identity becomes a "golfer." When we play poorly or post a bad score, it is logical that our "self" takes a hit, too.

Why Mental Toughness Training?

"The will to prepare is greater than the will to win." —Bobby Knight

Coach Vincent, NCAA coach of the year in 1999, has won forty-three tournaments as head coach at Washington University, UCLA, and Duke University combined. At the beginning of each season, he discussed with his collegiate golfers how every player who has reached the Division I level believed that his way of playing and preparing was the only way that worked. Because Coach Vincent encountered this attitude often, he reiterated the importance of building mental toughness.

Mental toughness has a variety of definitions and personal meanings, such as bouncing back, being resilient, persevering, etc., but this book encompasses mental toughness into two distinct components:

- Coping with struggle

- Performing well under pressure

This book is intended to build mental toughness through *how we prepare.* In order for us to become mentally tough, we should establish practices and competitions that allow us to cope with struggle and perform well under pressure.

There is a vast difference between golf and most other sports in terms of the challenges faced. Athletes in physically painful sports know that they will *hurt* at some point during the competition. Swimmers know that their body will be burning during the last twenty-five meters. Runners know their legs will feel like "Jell-o" during the last kick, and cyclists know that their lungs will soon enough be on "fire." Consequently, these types of coaches and athletes train the body to push past their current physical thresholds in order to handle and overcome the pain in competition.

Whereas golfers may face some physical challenges, their main obstacles are most often mental challenges, for the sport is so technically driven. In golf, the major mental challenges are playing golf swing not golf, losses of proper focus, and result-oriented thinking. However, most golfers rarely address training for these mental challenges. Their practice regimen consists of grooving swings and putting strokes with little or no devotion to developing mental toughness.

While athletes in physically painful sports know that they will encounter pain, golfers may actually believe that they will not face mental challenges during competitions. They often think that if their golf swing is developed properly, then they won't need mental training. However, all golfers can benefit from building mental toughness.

Few great golfers will earn their living playing professional golf. The route of "making a living" playing professional golf is honestly a sadistic journey. Playing well in the final stage of qualifying school (Q-school) is one of the only routes to the PGA Tour. The sport offers no guarantees and only limited reimbursement contracts. Golf makes no distinctions based on swing, equipment, type of school, and everyone has to pay to play. In professional golf specifically, one's amateur career is unimportant, and it makes no difference if someone previously won the United States Amateur or U.S. Amateur Public Links championship. Players can be extremely out of shape, have a horrible diet, smoke, and even drink excessive amounts of alcohol. The sport of golf holds no bias toward what anyone wears, how they act, or how they speak. Unfortunately, you can also have the dullest personality or just be a plain jerk. Of course, desirable and virtuous qualities are important to being a good person, but they are not required for success.

There are only two requirements for success in golf at any level: (1) executing golf shots and (2) making putts. While these are the only skills needed, the issue is timing, and these skills must be executed when it matters most. Birdie putts can't only be dropped on the front-nine, and low rounds mustn't be limited to casual rounds. The execution of golf shots and putts must be achieved during pressure moments. Similar to regular home golf matches, the bet really only matters when we press or the bet is pressed against us. Herein lays the paradox, because most practice is set up to pursue greatness through perfecting the golf swing. A lack of mental toughness (no matter how pretty the swing) won't allow the golfer to execute when needed most.

Searching or Practicing?
"The goal is to be physically loose and mentally tight."
-Arthur Ashe

Randy Wylie, PGA professional and volunteer coach at the University of Tennessee, was a consummate journeyman professional. After he played at Texas A&M, he played on various tours for nine years and even made the cut at two U.S. Opens. At dinner one evening, he spoke at length with Camilo Villegas during the beginning of Camilo's career on the PGA tour. While at Florida, Camilo's team won the NCAA championship, so Randy Wylie asked Camilo how *he* made it to the PGA tour while his teammates were playing on the Nationwide and mini-tours.

Camilo Villegas understood the parts of his game that he needed to execute properly to play well. He explained that when he played poorly, he examined what he did incorrectly and returned to practice, but he also commented that he avoided changing swing mechanics or "searching" for a key. On the other hand, after his former teammates played poorly, they would "search" for and experiment with different swing cues or swings instead of practicing.

How many of us are searching for a perfect swing or cue more often than we are actually practicing? In golf, defeat will occur often, so we should examine our outlook on setbacks and recommit ourselves to practicing rather than searching.

The Human Taproot

"[Golf] is not about shooting a record-low score or playing your best every day. It's about getting it in the clubhouse if you don't have it."
—Sean O'Hair

-Hardiness-

The dandelion is an interesting plant. It is generally revered by young children, because it is plentiful and because it is one flower that they can play with instead of just admiring like most others. At the same time, it is hated by most homeowners, because they believe it is just an annoying weed. Regardless of one's attitude toward the dandelion, it is a very hardy plant. It sprouts very quickly in most types of soil, growing in many climates, with little or lots of rainfall. It also does not seem to need the approval of its owner to grow successfully.

Mental toughness is akin to the hardiness factor in plants, which is a plant's ability to survive in adverse growing conditions. The measurement of a plant's hardiness includes its ability to withstand *drought, wind, cold, and heat*. The process of gardeners developing strains of hardy plants and shrubs involves the process of "hardening" them to the elements. Ironically, the hardiest types of plants (i.e., weeds and dandelions) are usually the most undesirable to the typical homeowners.

The common trait among all hardy plants, however, is the taproot. The taproot looks similar to a carrot or turnip and grows vertically down as opposed to branching off horizontally. It distributes water where needed, and it makes the plant very difficult to displace, because it will continue to resprout. Thus, developing mental toughness begins with developing a human taproot.

A human taproot is a metaphor of mental toughness. The analogy of a taproot is effective because akin to mental toughness, it is unseen. Honestly, when we look at a tree or plant, we only focus on the branches, leaves, and perhaps the fruit. Unless you are a botanist, you will pay little attention to what you can't see, namely the taproot.

Coaches and commentators often label the human taproot as "the intangibles." These unseen qualities are often immeasurable, yet the intangibles and the strength of the human taproot determine the success of each particular player. In golf, most are only interested in what can be observed (e.g., how far they can hit the ball, the picture of putting stroke, and their overall swing), yet it is only a small piece of what differentiates good players from great ones. Just as the strength of the taproot is what ultimately determines the longevity of the plant, the real key to success lies in the unseen, the intangibles, and one's mental toughness. If the roots are not strong, then the plant and player will eventually submit to the conditions.

Endure Suffering
"Hidden in all misfortune is fortune."
—Lao-tzu

In the exceptional book, *Man's Search for Meaning*, Victor Frankl discusses how we find meaning in our lives. Victor Frankl was a prisoner of war in three different concentration camps during WWII. To summarize the story, he developed the notion that we find meaning in three ways: (1) *doing a deed*, (2) *experiencing a value*, and (3) *suffering*.[3] He illustrated the third point of meaning by telling how his wife died in the camps, and how his manuscript (a lifetime of work) was discovered years into his containment and destroyed. He had to recreate his experiences and write it only on stolen pieces of paper. In short, in order for us to build mental toughness, we also must suffer.

What do the football players of Ray Everett, Dennis Byrd, Mike Utley, and Jim MacLaren all have in common? Each was at the peak of his career (Jim Maclaren as the best one-legged triathlete) when he suffered quadriplegia accidents. All stated that they would not have changed the incident, and it was the best thing to happen. Research supports these claims and reveals that most able-bodied people would pay *more* to remain able-bodied than disabled people would to become able-bodied once again.[4]

Though the above heroes did suffer, they experienced tragedy firsthand whereas most of us can only imagine what it would be like. Those not caught in current dire situations overestimate how long they would suffer and feel awful from a possible dramatic event. [5] Alas, these difficult events for the aforementioned football players were merely moments in time, and after a period, their resiliency was able to come to the forefront. The truth is that negative events and suffering affect us, but not as bad as we might think. Although most argue that suffering is not needed, enduring suffering is necessary.

In an attempt to improve, progress, and properly reflect, we must suffer in practice and play. I don't think that we need paralysis in order to grow. But, the reality of life, sports, and golf is that suffering happens. It is unfortunate that bad events happen, but the longer we live, the more poor experiences we will inevitably encounter. We shouldn't fear loss or suffering that will occur. Similar to able-body people, we mustn't overestimate an event's importance or significance, because we then become mentally handicapped by the fear of the event. 2005 ESPY Arthur Ashe award-winner Jim Maclaren states, "Fear is a good thing. It means something good can happen."

Why do athletes cry during losses and victories? They realize how much suffering they have endured in practice and the sacrifices they have made, and they are often overwhelmed with emotion at that moment. If we are to experience these feelings of elation, we must endure feelings of inadequacy or loss. We must endure suffering as well. In the book, *In a Pit with a Lion on a Snowy Day,* author Mark Batterson summarizes the concept of suffering when he says, "Sickness helps us appreciate health. Failure helps us appreciate success. Debt makes us appreciate wealth. It is the bad days that make us really appreciate the good ones." [6]

Building Mental Toughness
"The things which hurt, instruct."
—Benjamin Franklin

Suffering is inevitable and unavoidable, so you should try to foster an environment in practice that enables suffering. Think of how many golfers at the beginning of each season want to win a tournament or championship? Yet most players only want it at their convenience and are not willing to suffer to achieve it. Practices must be created with goals that are difficult to achieve and also create feelings of frustration and fatigue. These moments of suffering will not only be encountered on the course, but also help create who we are.

Life and golf are especially difficult, requiring patience and dedication to reach one's goals. You *will* become tired and not perform well, and thoughts of quitting may enter; however, these are the critical moments suffering that you need to endure in order to grow. Here are just a few examples of athletes and historical figures who have endured suffering:

- Dan O'Brien (the favorite to win the Decathlon gold medal at the 1992 Barcelona Olympics) missed all attempts on the pole vault at the Olympic trials and went from first to last. He stated, "It was like a bad dream." His comeback culminated with winning the 1996 gold medal.

- Tim Mack (missed qualifying for the 2000 Olympics in the pole vault). He was ranked tenth in the world, qualified in 2004 at the Olympic trials and won the gold medal in Athens.

- Park Tae Hwan of Korea was fourteen years old when he was disqualified for an illegal start at the 2004 Olympic Games in the four hundred meter freestyle. He was so distraught that he stayed in a bathroom for hours. In 2008 at the Beijing Olympics, he won the gold in the race becoming the first to do so for Korea.

- Hayley McGregory finished third at the 2004 and 2008 U.S. Olympic trials four separate times, but only the top two finishers advanced to the Olympics. She did not advance to the Olympics despite setting the world record in the hundred meter backstroke. (The record was broken during the next race.)

- Silken Laumann was the favorite to win the 1992 gold medal in the single scull. Ten weeks prior to the games, another rowing scull cut across her, broke her leg, and shredded her muscles. Within ten days, she had five operations, and she was rowing just twenty-seven days after the accident. Not only did she row, she still won the bronze medal for Canada.

- Arguably the greatest shortstop of all time, the Ironman, Cal Ripken, holds the distinction of hitting into the most career double plays.

- Cy Young holds the all-time record for wins (over five hundred) yet also holds the all-time record for losses (over three hundred).

- Abebe Bikila won the 1960 Olympic marathon while he ran barefoot. He became the first African American to win the 26.2 Olympic race. When asked why he ran barefoot, he said, "I wanted the world to know that my country, Ethiopia, has always won with determination and heroism."

- During the 1976 Olympics in Montreal, Shun Fujimoto, a Japanese gymnast, broke his knee during a floor exercise, but he did not let on, knowing it could hurt his teammates' confidence. He recorded a 9.7 on the rings after an eight-foot dismount, his best score ever, to help Japan win the team gold.

- Arnold Palmer, "the king," had a seven-shot lead at the 1966 U.S. Open with nine holes to play. He ended up losing in a playoff to Billy Casper.

- Johnny Unitas's first pass was intercepted and returned for a TD.

- Mark Zupan was a college soccer player when he was in a car accident one night while he was riding in the backseat. He broke his neck and clung to a tree branch in chilly canal water for fourteen hours before he was rescued. He thrived as a Paralympics' champion and starred in the epic documentary, *Muderball*.

- Jim Maclaren was a college football player at Yale University. One night while he was riding his motorcycle in NYC, a bus struck his wheel, and he was pronounced DOA (dead on arrival). Ultimately, all he lost was his leg, and he transformed himself to become a champion in triathlons. In a race on a closed course, a van struck his bike and rendered him a quadriplegic. Because of his rehabilitation and immense pain, he developed an addiction to cocaine. He reformed himself once again, and now he is a speaker and founder of the Choose Life Foundation.

Suffering is inevitable, so we should orchestrate a practice environment that welcomes suffering. Ed Moses was a gold medalist in the 4x100 medley relay in the breaststroke at the 2000 Sydney games. His training regimen welcomed suffering through his practice. While he swam at the University of Virginia, he epitomized building mental toughness. He awoke and swam his 6:00 am workout covering 8,000 meters in the morning session. He then came home, ate, slept, and awoke for his 10:00 am session. He spread out this practice through the entire day by repeating the process four times and covering 32,000 meters total. In comparison to other "elite" level swimmers, who average 50,000 meters in a week.

The U.S. Navy SEALS (sea, air, and land) unit is the most elite level of special operation units in perhaps the entire U.S. Armed Forces. Richard

Machowicz, at six feet tall and 155 lbs., was an unlikely candidate to become a U.S. Navy SEAL and special ops sniper. In order to become a SEAL, each individual must endure Hell Week of BUD/S (Basic Underwater Demolition/SEAL training). Because under 7 percent of people who are qualified to become a U.S. Navy SEAL actually make it, Mack's chances were not good. He trained using unusual methods to build mental toughness for BUD/S. He would take ice cold showers to help him acclimate and control the negative voice in his head, which could potentially tell him to quit. During his training, he developed his mental toughness mantra of "I can only be defeated if I give up or die." [7] Richard Machowicz not only became a U.S. Navy SEAL, but he developed his own style of martial arts. Now he is the host of the show *Future Weapons*.

Swimming the English Channel is one of the most difficult endeavors that the human body can endure, and its difficulty is the reason that only 10 percent of people who attempt this feat actually make it. It is nineteen nautical miles (38,000 meters) of swimming. Water temperatures are between fifty-nine and sixty-five degrees Fahrenheit, and hypothermia is always an issue due to the ten to twenty hours of open water exposure. In addition, swimmers must avoid open sea rubbish and have a support team to help feed them appropriately. Because of the difficult task, swimmers often team together and take turns swimming (no easy task as well). Marcia Cleveland successfully swam the English Channel and discussed her mental toughness training in her book *Dover Solo*. She stated as advice, "Acclimate! Swim enough yardage. Swim in the dark. Swim in all the rough and cold (fifty-five degree) water you can find. Try out different feeds in salt water, and when you feel like not finishing, think of all the people who have supported your dream and tell yourself, 'Yes, I can.'" [8]

> *"Not only so, but we also rejoice in our suffering, because we know that suffering produces perseverance. Perseverance produces character. Character produces hope, and hope does not disappoint us, because God has poured out His love into our hearts." —Romans (Chapter 5, Verse 3)*

Perspective from Suffering
"Everyone wants to go to heaven, but no one wants to die."
—Peter Tosh

People remark that time flies after one has children. I have yet to hear someone say that it "moves along so slowly." Time really does not move along any faster with children, but what has changed is the perspective. Before, time and age was something we all could avoid, and we were usually only aware of time during our birthdays or other milestones. With children however, there is actually a time clock on life that becomes apparent. Perspective of time is frighteningly clear when one looks at his or her eight-month old, celebrates the first birthday, sends a child off to kindergarten, or watches a teenager grow up and get a license. Because of the process of having children, we are now more aware of time than ever before.

This is not a knock on society, but the mind simply does not allow us to formulate a proper perspective. For instance, only 6 percent of high-school athletes will compete collegiately, and less than 1 percent of the athletic population will actually make it to the professional leagues. However, there is an overwhelming mis-perception among most athletes in high school. The latest research from The University of Pittsburgh Medical Center (UPMC) estimates that 70 percent of high school athletes believe that they will play collegiately, whereas 17 percent expect to play professionally. Notwithstanding the fact that possessing the belief in oneself is necessary for success, the statistics illustrate that most either lack the idea of the talent level or how hard they have to work to "make it."

Suffering in practice allows us to develop perspective. The two principles of a proper perspective are the following:

- Gratitude

- Inconvenience

First, perspective through gratitude is a skill that we must continually cultivate and develop. For instance, Todd Demsey recently re-secured his PGA Tour card; however, he has twice had brain surgery to remove golf ball size tumors. Through his experience, he has maintained a proper perspective regarding his performance. He states, "I used to live and die on every shot. It's still my job. It's what I love to do. It's not quite as important to me as it was before all this. But I feel really lucky to be able to play golf for a living." [9]

Individuals who have expressed gratitude have usually been those who have experienced an injury. These instances of "forced" layoffs are usually the most difficult periods for competitive athletes. They have encountered the struggles of not being able to perform, and their appreciation of returning is usually tenfold. We can recall watching Tom Brady's knee injury against the Chiefs during the first game of the 2008 season, forcing him to sit out the entire year. "When I was playing every week, I bitched about the little things," Brady stated. His knee injury, however, forced him to develop a proper perspective. "So this year if I hear two-a-day practices—great! Let's have three … whatever you say, coach." [10] This also does not mean that we have to become injured in order to appreciate life, but injuries force us to develop a proper perspective.

Coach John Wooden understood the power of developing perspective. During key moments, instead of punishing his players by running them, John Wooden would actually withhold practice time from his players if they were not putting forth their best effort. The practices were notoriously difficult, and his players became *thankful* that they could even practice.

Secondly, perspective is enhanced by understanding that "it's only an inconvenience." The death of a loved one, major illnesses, and devastating natural disasters are examples of tragedies that affect us and those around us. It does not mean that we will suffer permanently; however, it does mean that our lives will be forever changed. In the proper place, everything else in life that is unfortunate is only an inconvenience. "It's not the end of the world. My dog will still lick my face whether I win or lose," said Matt Biondi, Olympic champion. [11] Regardless of how important golf becomes, it still remains a sport.

Start Strong ... Finish Strong ...

"No one who can rise before dawn three hundred and sixty days per year fails to make his family rich."
—Chinese proverb

An interesting activity is watching the end of a five or ten kilometer race. The most exciting part is the winning "kick" by the eventual champ. The ending is merely a reflection of who has trained the hardest or, as Steve Prefontaine stated, *"who has the most guts."* The second interesting facet usually isn't witnessed by most, but it consists of watching the actions of the top runners after races. They run! Of course, the post-run has physiological benefits of dissipating lactic acid buildup, but it also signifies the essence of competition and life, because there always is another race. The same principle applies to golf. There is always another shot.

Start Strong
-Don't let your strength become a weakness.-

We would not expect for anyone to workout a few days before a game or competition and expect it to improve their performance. However, it seems that gyms and health clubs across the country become packed every year right before spring break!

Advanced workout regimens focus on specific body parts and constantly vary in intensity, schedule, and exercises. Conversely, beginners at strength and performance training usually address all muscle groups during every workout, rarely varying either in intensity or exercises. Beginners also usually only attend to their strengths and comforts while they neglect their weaknesses. Any improvements in strength or weight-loss goals are barely noticeable, and motivation soon lulls.

Mental toughness training is comparable to physical and strength training. It takes patience and dedication to change the way one thinks, reacts, and behaves. However, some people think that one session with a sport psychologist before they go play will help. Just as we can't workout for a week before spring break and expect to see a difference, mental toughness training is also a long-term process that begins by starting strong and having a plan. The first step is to identify the strengths and limitations of your physical and mental game and develop a plan to address these aspects.

People often overlook the fact that *every strength is also a weakness.* Think, for example, about the strength of a youth golfer who can outdrive all opponents by thirty or forty yards. The weakness is that the short game or iron game will eventually suffer, because there is no immediate need to develop those facets. It is easier to practice our strengths, because it reinforces our confidence and makes us feel comfortable. Directing our attention to our weaknesses is much more difficult, because we are stepping out of our comfort zones. However, if we only rely on our strengths, then they will eventually become weaknesses. Mental toughness training is intended to change your weaknesses into your greatest strength.

Practice: Start Strong
-Get out of the gate.-

Coach Griffin, during his twenty-five-year tenure at Auburn University, won thirty-nine tournament titles and earned SEC coach of the year four times. The following competition was designed as a nine-hole round to emphasize "starting strong." Coach Griffin called the game "Get out of the gate" and he changed the scoring format during play that stressed the first three holes. At the end of play, an eighteen hole score would be posted, but the first three holes are counted (thrice), holes 4–6 are scored (twice), and holes 7–9 are counted once.

Finish Strong
-Make your weakness your greatest strength.-

In the movie, *Any Given Sunday,* Coach D'Amato (Al Pacino) summarizes the essence of athletics during his pregame speech before the last game of the season. He states, "Because in either game—life or football—the margin for error is so small. One half step too late or too early and you don't quite make it. One half second too slow, too fast and you don't quite catch it. The inches we need are everywhere around us." [12]

The only difference between a "great" putt and a "good" putt is that a great putt goes in the cup. Within golf though, it is a big difference, and all it takes is a good putt to just "drop" sometimes. The key to becoming mentally tough is being able to improve and to "fight for that inch" within practice. At *every* practice, we must strive to become just a little bit better and put forth the extra effort that is necessary.

Putting forth the extra effort necessary is outlined in the brief movie, 212 degrees. Author Sam Parker points out that water is extremely hot at 211 degrees; however, water boils and produces steam at 212 degrees, and steam can power a locomotive (visit the website *212 The Extra Degree Movie*).

We can improve by one degree if we make a commitment to *finish strong.* Whether it is completing a putting drill with ten makes in a row, holing out a bunker shot, or executing ten perfect shots in a row, finishing strong is one of the best ways of improving performance. Finishing strong helps ensure that we have put forth our best and provides a quality reference point for our next practice.

Practice: Finish Strong
-Get it in the barn.-

Another competition by Coach Mike Griffin at Auburn, "Get it in the barn", also consisted of a nine-hole round. This nine-hole competition for building mental toughness was designed for players to "finish strong." This time, holes 1–3 are counted only once. Holes 4–6 are counted (twice), and holes 7, 8, and 9 are counted (thrice). The emphasis on "finishing strong" requires the player to forget the past holes and keep the same focus throughout.

Practice Players and Game Players
"What are we talking about, practice?"
—Allen Iverson

There are two types of players: practice players and game-day players. Both types can be successful, but we must understand our type so that we can avoid our strengths becoming weaknesses. Practice players usually have the best sessions and workouts and seemingly spend the most amount of time working on their game (e.g., K. J. Choi, Vijay Singh, Paddy Harrington, among others). Practice players often enjoy the golf swing mentality on the range so much that they sometimes enjoy the solitude, peace, and comfort more than actually competing. At all levels, there are players who mention how they have worked harder than ever yet they are playing worse. If practicing is your strength, you must become more of a game-day player by continually reinforcing competition in practice.

On the other hand, there are players who may putt and chip a few balls and then want to "tee it up." These game-day players seem to have the "intangibles" of competing at a higher level during competition. Rickie Fowler is one of the best young players on the PGA Tour. During a tournament in 2009, before having some top ten finishes on the PGA, he finished second at the Nationwide Tour event in Columbus, Ohio. On the Monday of the tournament, he hit balls on the range for about fifteen minutes. He looked at his caddy and said, "I'm going to chip and putt." This was a player who understood his swing was great and didn't need to keep hitting balls.

Carlos Franco is another example of a game-day player. He has won four times on the PGA Tour and hasn't kept secret his malaise for practice. After winning the 2004 U.S. Bank Championship in Milwaukee, he commented that he spent the week fishing at a friend's pond. "When I came here in 1999, 100 percent no practice."[13] After shooting a sixty-six in the first round of the Deutsche Bank Championship, Franco elaborated on his disdain for practice on the range and said, "I hit. I hit. I hit. Every shot is the same."

Anthony Kim is a player not renowned for his practice habits. After the 2008 Ryder Cup and two PGA Tour victories, he admitted to becoming apathetic toward his game. Kim has confessed that during the off-season, he won't even touch a club. "[My game] it's mental. It's being prepared when I get here." [14] Anthony Kim is obviously a game-day player; in 2009, he set an unofficial Masters record with eleven birdies during the second round.

Which is more important—practicing or playing? Hopefully we don't relish in our practice habits so much so that we disregard performance. However, we can't only play golf and expect to reach our potential without devoting time to practice. In order to become mentally tough, we must combine both practice and competition. Assume responsibility for developing mental toughness by focusing on strengths while you develop your weaknesses.

The Four C's of Mental Toughness

The four C's provide a framework in which we can assess specific components of mental toughness:

- Control

- Commitment

- Challenge

- Confidence

In this book, *Control* addresses the psychological need for control in our lives, how giving up control actually gains control, how-to "play golf" not golf swing, and the importance of a go-to shot. *Commitment* refers to a strong belief in one's chosen endeavor and how we must answer "the question." *Challenge* attends to how we view situations and events, and focusing on the "game within the game." *Confidence* addresses specific paths of how we gain and lose our feeling of confidence.

Control

"Dogs don't bark at parked cars."
—Anonymous

Langer and Rodin (1976) conducted monumental research that examined the power of control in our lives. They used over a hundred residents within a nursing home where the average age of the residents was eighty years old. They all received a house plant, but the differences in control (high/low) were (1) whether or not they could choose their own plant and (2) whether or not they could care for the plant.

Those on the first floor were told that they could choose which plant they wanted and that they alone would be responsible for taking care of it (high control). Residents on the second floor were given their plant and told that the nursing home would take care of it (low control).

The results were astonishing. Residents who took care of their own plants were more active, had higher morale, and had less depression than the low-control group. Six months later, 30 percent of the low control residents had passed away, compared to only 15 percent of residents who took care of their own plant. It seems strange that something as simple as taking care of a plant could have such profound effects on one's disposition, activity level, and overall health, yet it reveals the underlying importance and psychological need for "control." [15]

Ian Woosnam hit a wayward shot thirty to forty yards off-line on the par three twelfth tee during the 1992 U.S. Open at Pebble Beach. He immediately turned to his caddy and said, "There is something wrong with that ball!" He honestly believed that there was something wrong with the ball. If he accepted that it had been his swing, then he may have had a harder time during the round trying to correct it. Sure enough, on the next tee box, he striped his drive down the middle of the fairway.

How people explain their successes and defeats is the window into their perception of control. Pessimists construct negative viewpoints devoid of control: "It's going to last forever. I am going to lose, and it's my fault." On the other hand, optimists view situations as temporary and ultimately controllable. For example, they may say, "It's just a mistake. It will be okay." Translated into golf speak, that means, "It is just a bogey or a bad round. I'll get it back."

Great players use *temporary* attributions. They are optimists because they say things like, "I had a bad day. Nothing would drop. We'll get 'em tomorrow," thereby enhancing their outlook, whereas pessimists will assume more permanent attributions, saying "One bad hole always messes up my round. I can't ever play well on this course," lowering one's perception of control.

Optimists believe that they get all the good bounces, whereas pessimists believe that they rarely, if ever, get the good breaks. When you get a good bounce during play, chalk it up to being the luckiest golfer, but when a bad bounce does happen, you still must remain optimistic. You must say, "That is so strange that I got a bad bounce, because I am the luckiest golfer there is."

Control or Influence
"In order to get control, we have to give up control."
—-Anonymous

There is a difference between what we can control and what we can influence. Often, however, we spend more time trying to influence what we can't control rather than perfecting what we can control.

The golf swing is eerily similar to our children. Children become the most important aspect of our life, whereas the golf swing is the most important part of our game. As parents, we may feel like we have control over our children, but the harsh reality is that all we have is influence. We can ask, demand, plead, threaten, nag, punish, reward, guilt, or even praise our children to do what we want them to do, yet these are all aspects of influence that contain the illusion of control. If we try to control our children, all is lost until we stop it. Also, the more we try to control others, the less effective we become. Oddly enough, if we give up control, then we actually gain more control.

As much as we would like to groove a perfect swing, we must realize the extent of our influence. Remarkably, when we trust our strokes and swings, we have more success than when we try to steer shots or guide our putts. Paradoxically, we gain more control when we give up control.

The *golf swing* is the staple of what we can influence. It is indeed the most important aspect when we execute golf shots, but other aspects are neglected as a result. Mentally tough athletes perfect the aspects that they can control. They spend the most amount of time preparing on aspects within their control:

- Attitude

- Pre- and post-shot routine

- Practice habits

- Course management

- Fitness levels

- Mechanics (stance, setup, and alignment)

Have we spent so much time trying to influence (or even control) our golf swing that we have neglected the aspects really within our own control? In order to develop mental toughness, it is not enough to merely pay homage to aspects within our own control. We must perfect *all* aspects within our control.

Again, the way to *get control is to give up control*. It is a paradox, but it is effective and allows one's talent to come through. The opposite of giving up control, however, is to get in our own way by playing golf swing, not golf.

Play Golf not Golf Swing

"We are what we repeatedly do. Success therefore becomes a habit."
—Aristotle

During this golfer's senior season in the early 1990s, his team won the NCAA golf championships. He decided to turn pro, even though anyone would have bet money that both of his teammates would have been more successful as professionals. His teammates were winners of the U.S. Amateur Public Links and top-ranked, junior players of the year respectively. In addition, during his first professional year in 1992, when the Nationwide Tour was dubbed the Ben Hogan Tour, the buzz on the circuit concerned his ugly swing, and people often asked, "How is he even out here?" Even though his teammates at Arizona, David Berganio Jr. (two-time U.S. Public Links champion) and Manny Zerman (Pac-10 Champ and two-time runner U.S. Amateur runner-up) were great golfers, they were not exactly household names yet. Despite that, 13-time PGA Tour winner and 2003 U.S. Open champ, Jim Furyk, has established a hall of fame career.

"We are what we repeatedly do—." What is practiced and, more importantly, how your practice is executed, will determine your most dominant trait. No one knew this better than Ben Hogan, perhaps the greatest ball-striker of all time. Ben Hogan stated that two components associated with playing great golf were a "repeatable golf swing" and "how bad are the misses."[16]

The range is where you should practice your "golf swing," and during a round is the time to trust the swing and "play golf." However, if the golf swing is all that is practiced, then during a round, your "golf swing" will be played. Of course, if the swing is great that day, then your "golf swing" will work, and mental toughness is not needed. The concern relates back to Ben Hogan's remark of "how bad are the misses." The tendency is for "golf swingers" to make adjustments during a round after some poor swings, which is a behavior that merely acts as a Band-Aid. Before long, the "golf swinger" is no longer executing golf shots, just trying to correct the swing. We can judge our natural tendency either to play "golf or golf swing" when faced with a forced carry over water. Water seems to do funny things to golfers, so when we are struggling with our game or faced with a tough shot, we revert to what we practice.

Why is there the tendency for golfers to play "golf swing" during a round? First, when placed under pressure, there is a tendency to revert to our normal practice habits. One of the top coaches in the world, Chuck Cook, labeled these habits as the *primacy* effect, meaning at some point, we revert to what and how we have practiced. When we only practice "golf swing," the primacy effect takes over, and we search for a swing key during pressure moments.

The other reason we revert to the "golf swing" during a round is that we are seeking to regain control. When playing well, our thoughts are so simple and clear and engrossed in the target that we don't even recognize our thoughts. These are the times that we are *giving up control*, however, when we start playing golf swing after some loose shots or poor holes, we feel the need to regain control. We attempt to regain control by "thinking" about our golf swing. It does not necessarily mean that our thoughts are negative; the thoughts may be instructional in nature, like keeping your knuckles down through the swing, but there is a level of automaticity with our game that more thoughts equates with a lack of trust in the execution of the skill.

Beilock, Carr, Macmahon, and Starkes (2002) examined the accuracy of putts by experienced golfers who were instructed to either think about their stroke or an auditory tone. Remarkably, the skilled golfers who attended to their swing performed worse than those who attended to the auditory tone. Case in point, golfers who "play golf" do better than golfers playing "golf swing."[17]

Quality practice will make the swing more repeatable, however, the issue is the "perfect" swing or putting stroke. There are so many moving parts in the swing that it makes perfection impossible, yet everyone can develop mental toughness within practice.

"Playing golf" must be emphasized during practice and sometimes even during our play.

Practice: Let Go Already
*-Try playing by pretending that this round is actually
for real … After all one can care too much. –*

Only when someone is able to play without worrying about the results can he or she play without inhibition. There are two strategies for developing this attitude: (1) Play, as if it was practice, or (2) Practice, as if every shot mattered.

Bob Christinia of UNC-G and Eric Alpenfels of Pinehurst conducted a study for *Golf Magazine* in which golfers looked at the hole while they putted. Participants were separated into two groups. The control group putted normally, and the experimental group was instructed to look at the hole while they putted. The results indicated that on putts between twenty-eight to forty-three feet, the group looking at the hole was nine inches closer (24 percent closer) to the hole than the control group. [18]

While we will probably never putt this way during competition, it is important to utilize the following drill in practice and during casual rounds. The key is simple: *Look at the hole while you putt.* Obviously, practice is needed on the putting green prior to play. The drill is best performed by making sure your putter is lined up correctly and by keeping the ball in your peripheral vision. Try it right now as you are reading this. Put your hand over the sheet of paper and look at a spot on the wall in front of you. Can you still see your hand?

You must give up control in order to get control. This drill is intended for you to trust your line and "let go" of the putt. It is nearly impossible to focus on the stroke when your attention is already taxed. Pick your line, trust the speed, and let it go.

Practice: Second Ball Drill
"Alfred says to Tiger, 'How many shots do you want?'"
—Brenden Pappas

Who is Alfred? The above quote is relevant because Alfred is the second ball. How often is the second ball played exactly the way we want? The result of missing the shot has already occurred, so there are no thoughts or anxiety about the shot, and thus, we end up performing the way we intended. One way to practice *giving up control* is by playing an entire round, as if it was the second ball. We get out of our own way and just execute golf shots. It takes some practice pretending that it is a second ball, but what we discover about ourselves is how much better we can perform while we don't become preoccupied with the outcome.

Practice: Point and Shoot
"Aim small ... miss small."
—Mel Gibson

Because mechanics and "golf swing" can easily creep into our play, they can be monitored with another drill for *giving up control*. Play an entire round with the concept of "point and shoot."

Make sure that a big target is selected. This target should be a tree, a section of fairway, a house, or a sign marker. Let the mind process the information for a second. After a target is picked, make it smaller! Pick out a specific leaf on the tree, a window of the house, or a corner of the sign marker. After the smallest possible target is chosen, -point and shoot, - and the entire round should be played this way. If this is your normal style, then it will reinforce how you already play. Thus, the goal is to make sure that the smallest possible target is picked out before every shot! On the other hand, if this style of play is uncomfortable, then stay with it and avoid swing thoughts or mechanics. After some practice, it will become easier to "let it go."

This style of play is also intended to incorporate the "absence of a pre-shot routine." In order for something to feel comfortable, we have to sometimes make it feel uncomfortable. The "point and shoot" drill forces us to trust our target and our swing. Not having any routine because of "point and shoot" also reinforces the quality aspects in our normal pre-shot routine. Thus, when we return to our original pre-shot routine, it should feel more comfortable.

Actually play an entire round with this new style. Later on, when you notice that you have begun to think too much or that you are analyzing swing or stroke mechanics, put this style into action. This style of play does not mean that you don't care. It simply means that you trust yourself enough to give up control. As long as you have played with this style, it will be easier to revert to it when needed.

Go-To Shot
-Swing du jour.-

Tom Watson, at the 2009 British Open, was in the middle of the fairway on the eighteenth, and most every sports writer started to write how this was going to be the greatest victory by anyone ever. Needing a par to win, he was faced with wind at his back, and coupled with the adrenaline of the situation, he took an 8-iron (too much club in hindsight), hit a great shot, but it pitched forward and off the green. Eerily similar during the following weekend, Rickie Fowler, needing a par to win, was leading by one shot on the eighteenth at the 2009 Nationwide Children Hospital Invitational at Ohio State's golf course. He was just off the fairway in the rough, and similar to Tom Watson, he hit a great shot (just too much club) that pitched forward and off the green.

We must know what type of shot we can pull off under any lie, any wind, over water, and any situation. These moments require a confident "go-to" swing. During every round, there most likely will be five or six shots that require a precise execution. This could be a forced carry over water, a tight tee shot, or a tucked away pin. In the same manner during every round, there may be at least a few five-foot putts. The emphasis within practice should be to develop the "go-to shot" to help withstand pressure moments. These types of shots are developed through playing golf. When pressure mounts, we must know our tendencies.

Practice: Go-To Shot
"Center of the green never moves."
—Boo Weekley

At the 2006 Chattanooga Classic, I spoke at length on the practice green with Boo Weekley. Prior to first meeting a year earlier in 2005, Boo Weekley was a journeyman who fluctuated between the PGA and Nationwide Tours. He was a good ol' boy player, a great ball-striker who couldn't just quite get it all together. He has since won twice on tour, had stellar 2008 Ryder Cup play, and rose to the top twenty-five in the world; however, in 2005, he had just begun his ascent of stellar play.

Because Boo had started to play so well, I ventured to ask him one of the most important questions: how? He became quite serious while he answered and talked about his rededication to practicing. (Boo was known to utilize his fishing equipment the days prior to the tournaments.) As we talked, he was specific about what he did to improve his play.

Boo stated, "I worked really hard on my ten- to fifteen-foot putts [in the off-season]. I feel I should be able to make these and only fired at maybe four pins during the round." The Chattanooga Classic is a great tournament with low scores to be had by the players. For instance, the "cut" line has been around six under par with the eventual champ playing fifteen to twenty under par for four days. As I listened to Boo state that he *only* went at four pins, I thought that was absurd at the time. However, he mentioned some genius logic that day. He stated, "The center of the green never moves."

In order to develop a go-to shot, course management and the center-of-the-green mentality is crucial. First, one must commit to his or her "go-to" shot, which is easier with no trouble spots. However, sometimes doubt arises, and these thoughts cause extra tension in the hands or arms, which results in poor execution. Unfortunately, doubt can even creep into the mind at the last second, causing one to "bail" on the shot.

When we encounter doubt, we must decide on a center-of-the-green approach. Next, an aggressive swing should be the outcome. Times of confidence and of passive targets are just two instances of when it is easier to swing aggressively. If we have developed a go-to shot, it is a bonus when it fades or draws into the target, but a center-of-the-green shot won't hurt.

Often, instances of poor execution are the impetus of a poor game plan and have little to do with one's ability. These times of poor execution are incorrectly deciphered by the player as a poor swing with little reflection on the preceding game plan.

The center-of-the-green mentality allows us the most opportunities to make ten- to fifteen-foot putts. Also, it is mentally easier without the undue stress, overanalyzing, and painful critique with negative outcomes. Golf is hard enough. When in doubt about your go-to shot, remember the center of the green never moves!

Commitment

"Nothing is really work, unless you would rather be doing something else."
—James M. Barrie

The Tomb of the Unknown Soldier has been guarded twenty-four hours a day, seven days a week, since 1930. Guarding the tomb is considered an elite honor, but only a few are able and can endure the stringent requirements. First, guards commit to two years of service, and they must live in a barracks underneath the tomb. For the first six months of service, they cannot speak to anyone and spend off-duty time learning the 175 notable members buried in Arlington National Cemetery. They march in specific twenty-one step arrangements and change guards every thirty minutes for twenty-four hours a day. Guards dress themselves in front of a full-length mirror and often spend five hours cleaning and preparing their uniform. Guards cannot drink alcohol or swear in public for the rest of their lives. After two years of duty, each guard is presented with a wreath pin and must obey certain criteria for the rest of their lives or surrender the pin. Presently, there are approximately four hundred wearers.

The Western States Endurance run is a hundred-mile ultra-run and one of the oldest and most challenging trail running events. It is a trek from Squaw Valley to Auburn, California, consisting of rugged conditions and varying mountain ascents and descents accessible only by foot, horseback, or helicopter. The race begins at 5:00 AM, and all finishers must complete the journey by 11:00 AM the following day, so most of the running is completed at night. Altogether, physical, mental, physiological, and environmental hazards are encountered during this race. Even though runners must prove their worthiness and submit past race results to qualify, only approximately 60 percent finish the race each year. Lastly, the reward provided to all finishers is a belt buckle.

The Texas Water Safari is a 260-mile canoe race. It's moniker of the "world's toughest canoe race" seems appropriate, because the boaters race nonstop for thirty-six hours or more, and the goal is to never let the boat stop. Participants battle extreme heat, head winds, sleep deprivation, alligators, sharks, water moccasins, and copperheads. Canoeists have often reported hallucinations because of the extreme race as well. Those who finish the grueling trek receive a T-shirt and a meal at the end.

The Self-Transcendence Race is a 3,100 mile run. Runners begin each day at 6:00 AM and usually go until midnight, and they are supported by friends and handlers supplying food and supplies during each day. The race is not completed across stretches of land, either. Participants must circumnavigate a half-mile course around a building 5,649 times! The latest winner completed the journey in forty-six days and six hours. One runner, Suprabha Beckjord, completed the race eight times for a total of 24,801.37 miles. Beckjord stated, "Most people, if they are not into ultra-distance, they think … [it is] not even possible." The prize at the end of this arduous journey is a trophy and a photo album. No prize money is awarded. [19]

The Kaihigyo are spiritual athletes from the Tendai sect of Buddhism. They are better known as the marathon monks of Mt. Hiei. Their quest consists of a mere thousand-day challenge which takes more than seven years to complete. The running is completed in increments of a hundred days. Thus, the monks run a marathon every day up to six months at a time. After the first five years, the running becomes serious.

During the last two years, the monks complete two marathons a day, for a hundred consecutive days. Since 1885, only forty-six monks have completed the challenge. The conditions are quite severe as well. They begin running at midnight, trekking through mountain passes, and running in straw sandals (eighty pairs per hundred days) and white robes. They live on a diet of vegetables, tofu, and miso soup. The pilgrimage is so sacred that if they fail to finish, then they must hang or disembowel themselves. At the end of the journey, many citizens arrive hoping to be blessed by the monk completing the journey, but other than that, the finish is rather anticlimactic from an outsider's perspective. At the end of the journey, the monks are declared a "saintly master of the highest practice." [20]

These examples have a few common traits, namely the dedication and mental challenges of completing such tasks. However, the main ingredient amongst these events is the underlying motivation-the commitment. We can ascertain from the meager or lacking rewards offered for these events that these dedicated individuals were not driven by external factors. Participants were not solely motivated by money, scholarships, or contracts. In order to achieve these incredible feats, the motivation must have come from within. Once each of these people committed to the goal, their commitment was then challenged every day as they made the choice to train and "push" throughout training. The vast majority of these individuals did not wake up the morning of the journey and decide to "just do it."

The Question: Why do I practice, and why do I play?

Assess your underlying motivation by asking two questions: *Why do I practice, and why do I play?* We must be able to honestly assess our level of commitment, and it must be asked of ourselves during appropriate times. Making the turn after having bogeyed the last few holes is not the time to ask of ourselves, "Why am I out here?" During tough practices is not the time to self-reflect with rhetorical questions about our inner drive, either. If we can answer the "why" to the above questions, then we can come up with the "how."

First and foremost, playing must be fun. If it is not fun, then there really is no point to trying to improve your play. However, within any chosen endeavor, a love-hate relationship often develops. We love to win and play well, but at the same time, we hate to lose and play poorly. A successful executive once told me that he could practice and play to a three handicap or he could never practice, try to have fun, and play at a ten index. We have to ask these questions, because it is our journey and choice to devote to training and improving our game.

Jimmy Connors once stated, "I hate to lose more than I love to win." Similarly, there are two options to any type of endeavor. We can train to do our best, or we can train very minimally and just be a "participant." To be content with the participant mindset is similar to the "love to win" mentality. Who doesn't love to win? However, actually winning seems to take more than a "love to win" mentality. Through my work, I have noticed that the real motivation of champions stems from a standpoint of "hating to lose." These players want to "know" that they are ready as opposed to just "hoping" that they are ready. In return, they refuse to leave any stone unturned in their quest for greatness.

There is a solution of balancing the love-hate relationship and of answering the question of why we play and practice. On tour, I repeatedly ask golfers their favorite aspects of playing. The most common answer is "competition." I agree! Pitting oneself against another is truly a great feeling. However, competition is merely an assessment of how well we measure up. Along with the aforementioned marathons, tests of will, and dedicated professionals, the competition ultimately is against oneself.

Competition in golf and life is a process against oneself. We should devote our time to seeing how good we can become. While there may be various goals or results that we desire, the focus should be on the actual process of execution both physically and mentally. If the process is executed properly, then results will eventually take care of themselves. Oftentimes, we can get caught up with thinking about perfecting the swing or driving the ball further, but when the focus becomes solely result-oriented, like beating an opponent or outdriving a player, then we must return to the questions: *Why do I practice? Why do I play?* On the other hand, if we set a goal of winning a tournament, although it involves results, it can set us on a course of working on ourselves and our game to achieve this goal. We can then answer the questions more easily.

Why Are They Champions?
"You can't push a rope."
—Anonymous

How could a person who was seventh on the depth chart as a quarterback in college and drafted in the sixth round at #199 overall become one of the best professional quarterbacks? Before you begin any type of preparation/training, you must make certain that you are committed. The best competitors at every level reach deeper and prepare themselves better than everyone else. Future hall of fame quarterback, Tom Brady, became one of the best because of his work-ethic and ability to recognize his weaknesses and distractions.

Commitment is not one huge event. It is a lot of small decisions and matches. It will take pushing through tough loses, almost makes, and continually answering the question *why I practice and play?* Commitment must be constantly revisited every day because it is *you* who must choose to face the hours of dedication.

Is your level of commitment strong enough to endure outside questioning and ridicule? British Open winner Tom Lehman was not even recruited by one college team, yet he displayed commitment. He stated, "You haven't been a golf pro if you haven't slept in your car." Mark Hensby's persistence is also noteworthy. He lived out of his car and sold insurance for his expenses. [21] [22]

Colt Knost, as an amateur in 2007, won both the U.S. Public Links and the U.S. Amateur tournaments. Along with helping the United States win the Walker Cup, he accomplished all he could as an amateur. The spoils of victory from the Public Links and U.S. Amateur are invitations to both Open Championships and the Masters. However, instead of relying on sponsorship exemptions, he turned pro and forfeited playing in the majors for a chance at Q-school. Although he received some ridicule from a few of the game's purists, Knost remarked, "I'll be back there one day. I am happy with my decision. " [23] Perhaps his level of commitment helped him achieve his goals, for he won twice on the Nationwide Tour in 2008 and earned his PGA Tour card.

Practice: Commitment
-In order to achieve something great, something must be given up-

A few questions to assess your current motivation include the following:

1. *What are your individual goals for the season?*

2. *What is your strategy to achieve these goals?*

3. *Who will you share these goals with? Who will hold you accountable?*

4. *What are you willing to sacrifice in order to achieve this goal?*

Challenge Your Commitment

"Security is mostly a superstition; it does not exist in nature. Life is either a daring adventure or nothing."
—Helen Keller

What causes us pain on the course and how do we stay committed to the goal? First, begin by noting the most frustrating situations:

- Missing a short putt

- Making a bogey from the fairway

- Not taking the range out with you on the course

- Misplacing a wedge

- Bogeying a par five

- Three-putting

- Not converting up and down

- Being in a greenside bunker

- Double-bogeys

Make sure you cite a specific example and not something general. Now assess whether it is something within your control. Do you become frustrated by external factors like the following:

- Poor greens

- Slow play

- Weather delays

- Coaches

- Playing partners

Anger and frustration are the most common responses, and though these are normal responses, the solution is to become better rather than normal. However, anger and frustration aimed at *ourselves* is the worst, because it is accompanied by perfectionism, hurtful thinking, resentment, self-rejection, and self-doubt.

All of these thoughts in competition dwell on *you* as the problem, and these types of thoughts make it much more difficult to let go of a mistake, hurting your chances of a successful next shot. Thus, you must introduce practices and competitions that challenge your commitment.

Practice: Committing to the Shot
-We must properly understand what we already know.-

While caddying on tour, I'll help my player commit to the shot by having him announce precisely what the shot is going to do. Often by stating what we are going to do, we ignite the dormant forces, commit to the shot, and make it happen. This drill is intended to be transferred onto the course of play and the goal is to achieve the following three-step process for every shot, chip, and putt.

1. The player must announce *aloud* the planned ball flight and specific target.

2. At no time is the player allowed to criticize oneself for a bad swing.

3. The player is not allowed to think in-between shots about his or her swing.

4. If playing a course is difficult, then on the range, the player must do this for *ten consecutive shots*. The player should also go through his or her full routine before each shot and say the specific target aloud and announce the ball flight.

Practice: What's in Front of You?
"Don't look behind you, something might be gaining."
—Satchel Paige

Coach at the University of Illinois and 2009 PGA Professional national champion, Mike Small, has his team practice the maxim of "what's in front of you." If players are focused on the target and what lies ahead, then they avoid getting caught up with technique.

Coach Small instills "playing golf" by having his team play using only one club during practice to emphasize distance control through low, medium, and high shots. He will also drop coins on the fringe of the green and ask his players to hit the targets consecutively. The University of Illinois golf team also has competitions around the green with nontraditional clubs like a 5-iron to emphasize, "shot-making."

Practice: Hit the Green
-Be comfortable, being uncomfortable-

Coach Mike Griffin had his players practice "playing golf" by placing the emphasis on "hitting the green." During actual play, if they were on the green in regulation, then they could finish the hole normally; however, if they missed the green, then they had to drop it in a greenside bunker and play it out from there.

Practice: Head for Head/Shot for Shot
"When elephants fight, it's the grass that suffers."
—Kikuyu proverb

Another competition is titled "head to head/shot for shot." This game is accomplished on the range. The goal is similar to playing "horse" in basketball. One must call his or her shot, and the next player must match it or receive a letter. Not only must one shape shots with different clubs and trajectories in order to win, but as a result of the pressure, one learns his or her "go-to shot." This game can even be transferred into actual play when a player calls the shot and the opponent must match it or else receive a letter or a stroke. Having players experiment with various shots (e.g., stinger 6-irons, closed feet tee shots, and 30-yard bump and runs) cultivates playing golf by testing these shots in actual play.

Practice: Draw-Straight-Fade
"Those who cannot remember the past are doomed to repeat it."
—George Santayana

Todd Smith, former all SEC player at Auburn, professional at Rock Hollow Golf Club in Indiana, and brother of PGA Tour player Chris Smith, teaches his players to "play golf." He has a drill in which players must first execute a draw, then a straight shot, then play a cut, three times in a row. From this drill, he will then have his players play "cuts" or "draws" on the course for the entire round.

Challenge or Threat

"The only easy day was yesterday."
—U.S. Navy SEAL commandment

Zach Johnson commented that he didn't get nervous coming down the stretch during the 2007 Masters. Instead, he said that he was excited. Now, everyone gets nervous, but the key is how he or she perceives the situation. People either perceive events as challenges or threats. Missed putts, missed cuts, lost tournaments, poor ball striking, pushed drives, rain delays, lost balls, bad rulings, and slow play are all events that will eventually happen, but how we view these events will determine our course of action.

Viewing events as challenges is why the "greats" in any sport (e.g., Tiger Woods, Jack Nicklaus, Martina Navratilova, Wayne Gretzky, and Michael Jordan) thrive during pressure situations. Mental toughness enables people to see events and situations as opportunities instead of threats. It is the attitude that people "want" the ball at the end of the game. You must want the challenge of a five-foot putt to win a tournament.

View *all* events as challenges as opposed to threats. For instance, Ronda Rousey, the 2008 Olympic bronze medalist in judo, transformed herself by developing mental toughness. After she took a two-week hiatus from practice and coaches, she was forced into competing for prize money and stipends. "I had to compete well or else I wasn't going to eat," she said. "[I] went from this person who wants to win this tournament so they can have a nice weekend to I want to win so I can have pancakes on Wednesday." [24] In Beijing 2008, she became the first U.S. woman to ever medal at the Olympics in the sport of judo.

Game Within the Game
"Being on the tightrope is living; everything else is waiting."
—Karl Wallenda

Becoming mentally tough in golf requires that one focus on the immediate challenge as opposed to the results. A cliché in sports that coaches often use to accentuate the challenge is to "win the game within the game." Coach O.D. Vincent's goal for his players was to "bring their best" at every practice. It seems that this is a similar goal to many collegiate programs. He coaches that achieving this goal is dependent upon providing continuous competition within practice and play. He established a point system for competition that encouraged mental toughness, enhanced proper focus, and also afforded life skills training. The goal of an established point system compels players to continually improve because of the tangible outcomes. Thus, he composed a point-value system based on the premise that players could earn points in all aspects of their practice, schoolwork, and play. The point system is similar to the European Tour Order of Merit or the PGA Tour money list. One difference from the professional tours is that playing performance is not the only aspect rewarded. Points are also earned through effort and teamwork. Coach Vincent explained that, "If a teammate is doing everything right, he will earn a spot."

The life skills component of the point system is conveyed through the points that one earns. The environment for the golf team member resembles the life as a professional golfer. Coach Vincent provided each player with opportunities to get to know themselves as much as possible by "being your own boss." Players must understand what positives are in their lives and what negatives constitute distractions. Hence, the points are used as a form of currency that players must spend wisely. For instance, analogous with life, a player may want swing lessons with his pro, so he is required to "spend" a set amount of points.

Ball State University's coach, Mike Fleck, awards a travel spot to the individual who practices the best and completes specific performance tasks during the fall season. Regardless of how one performs during qualifying rounds or in actual competition, any player can earn a spot. Thus, to ensure players are practicing smart, he constructed a points system solely based on practice.

Points could be earned in the followings ways:

- walking thirty-six holes in one day

- winning short-game competitions

- holing out a bunker shot

Because specific performance criteria were based on aspects crucial for successful play, he also awarded "playing" points in other ways:

- having less than thirty putts in a round

- shooting a round in the sixties

- not having consecutive bogeys

Similarly, head baseball coach, Tim Corbin at Vanderbilt University, challenged his players to continually improve through competition. In his point system, his players were required to focus on the process of competition. In the past years, Vanderbilt baseball has established itself as a national power. Former players and current MLBers Pedro Alvarez and David Price were crucial to the success of the program. Thus, Coach Corbin's challenge has been to provide ways for his better players to improve.

One way he provided challenges was to construct intersquad games that build mental toughness by stressing the importance of competition, effort, teamwork, and "doing the small things" correctly. Coach Corbin stated, "If score is associated with it, then [David Price] will do anything he can to win." As a result, Vanderbilt's intersquad games were set up with points scored on a variety of aspects. Not only do runs count for score, but Coach Corbin adds points for many situational aspects, such as moving runners over with less than two outs, hitting cutoff men, holding men on base, limiting errors in the field, and successfully executing bunts. He emphasizes competition by adding points to pressure situations, too. For example, a pitcher and batter with a 3–2 count counts as a potential point to be scored by whoever wins the small battle. He emphasizes effort by including points for making sure everyone runs on as well as off the field. Coach Corbin highlights teamwork by awarding points if everyone is involving themselves, cheering, and encouraging other players. To reiterate, these aspects that coach Corbin sets forth forces his players to focus on the process of playing baseball as opposed to the final score.

Practice: Game within the Game
"How do you eat an elephant? One bite at a time."
—Bill Hogan

Remaining focused on the process becomes increasingly difficult the more often we have thoughts about the score. If thoughts of what one wants to shoot enter the mind at the beginning of the round, midway through, or during the last few holes, the introduction of these thoughts can cause a change in focus. These changes in focus can affect even the most talented of athletes.

During Tom Glavine's bid for win number three hundred, he was spotted a 6–0 lead even before he took the mound in the first inning. Glavine stated, "You get a big lead, but you have to say to yourself. Don't change the plan. Pitch like you would normally pitch. Of course the minute you do that, you aren't thinking the way you normally think." [25] Because there is such a natural tendency to focus on the final score, we must develop a focus that enables us to entertain these types of thoughts while we remain focused on the process.

The "game within the game" accomplishes an important aspect of setting goals, because it provides a clear vision of what is important, which in turn leads toward posting a good score. Research has shown that setting process goals is effective because it mobilizes effort and prolongs persistence. [26]

Because each player is different, there may be certain aspects that we feel are more important to the process of scoring. Some players may struggle with anger and letting go of shots, negatively affecting the next few holes. As a result, it is important to set up strategies for keeping score that address letting go of shots.

Practice: PGA Player's Game within the Game
"If you don't have some bad loans, you are not in business."
—Paul Volcker

The following process goals were designed for a touring pro trying to replace result-oriented thinking with a focus on the process. Research states that we are more likely to adhere to a program if we can *lose* money for not adhering rather than *gain* money for participating.[27] To elaborate, this concept of *loss aversion* states that some people will lose more satisfaction over losing $100.00 than they will gain from winning $100.00 when they are determining choices. Consequently, this PGA player would create incentive with himself in terms of making a "bet." He would wager $100.00 on himself every time he would play, and if he was over par (see below), he would lose the money (to me). This strategy was effective because it forced him to focus on the process and on the "game within the game." After about ten rounds of paying out, he was determined not to lose any more money.

-1 for every positive
1. *Bouncing back from bogeys with a par or better*
2. *Finishing my round with a par or better*
3. *Getting up and down from fifteen yards*
4. *Making birdie putt outside of five feet*
5. *Keeping my emotions on an even keel through good and bad holes (ONLY ONE POINT POSSIBLE)*

+1 for every negative
1. *Misclubbing*
2. *Taking unreasonable gambles (Course management)*
3. *Making poor decisions off tee*
4. *Remaining angry after next shot*
5. *Getting too excited (outcome thinking)*

Practice: Stop-Play
-Time-out-

Research shows that "icing" the kicker (calling timeout) in professional football is not significantly different in terms of outcome than not calling timeout. However, head coaches will always do so, because they can. One truism in golf is that at some point in the round, play will become slow, so it mustn't derail our momentum. One mental toughness drill is to "stop play" for five minutes at the turn, which is intended to mimic a real tournament situation. Whether the players perceive this unexpected delay as a challenge or a threat determines how they usually respond.

Stack the Deck
"We're not working on our game, we're working on ourselves."
—Geoff Ogilvy

In Vegas, you can find two types of people: those with a winner's mentality and those with a loser's mentality—the winner or loser's mentality relates to how one merely approaches the game. A loser mentally sits down at the table and states, "I am going to play until my money is gone," whereas a winner states, "I am going to play until I double my stack." They all have a plan, but they vary greatly in their approaches.

Scott Stallings and Chip Sullivan vary greatly in the golfing world. Chip has played successfully on all levels as a golf professional for many years, and Scott is a rising star as a professional golfer. Nevertheless, they both develop mental toughness through the competitions in which they play.

First, they both *refuse match play formats against opponents*, because it does not help the overall mentality like in stroke play. A mistake (e.g., three putt, not getting up and down) in stroke play is inherently more difficult to let go. Also, because they both play in local games against accomplished players, the level of competition is fairly strong, but while at home or during practice rounds, they do something that places their level of concentration at its peak. They *stack the deck against themselves!*

Stallings and Sullivan make the bet lopsided so that it forces them into not only good play but stellar play to win. Moreover, they offer limited betting terms so that they stand to lose much more money than they can actually win. These players realize that winning these games is not the goal; their goal is to prepare themselves for tournament play.

Practice: Stack the Deck
-Press the bet-

A way that any golfer can stack the deck is to "press." Basically, whenever down, announce quickly that you'll press the bet, regardless of the game or amount. It encourages mental toughness by naturally forcing one to play well on the next hole. Even if you are the one pressing or being pressed, these are the moments that are needed during actual competition.

The Five Paths to Confidence

"I know that they know that they know that I know I will win."
—Phil Parkin

What do the stars in the movies *Alien, The Patriot*, and all the *James Bond (007)* movies have in common? Sigourney Weaver, Mel Gibson, and Daniel Craig are all extremely confident. Because they are the stars, they realize that they are not going to die no matter what happens. In *The Patriot*, Mel Gibson makes a bold move when he grabs the American flag and runs back up the hill to fight. Of course, it's a movie, but confidence should be more like a movie anyway. Real life demonstrates that we are going to fail more often than we are ever going to succeed, so if we listen to real life, it will obviously become tougher to be confident.

Even when Arnold Palmer was a caddy in his youth, his friends commented about his confidence. As they played in their "fantasy" matchups, playing as Sam Snead, Bobby Jones, or Walter Hagen, Arnold Palmer actually played as "himself."[28]

We create our own reality and level of confidence. Similar to the movies, we need to adopt a star role. Now, the current day "American Idol" mindset has many thinking that everyone can be a star, and due to the crying after the first round of cuts, obviously, some individual's perceptions are a bit skewed. However, within our chosen passion, there are three facets of confidence:

- **Confidence is a feeling**

    When we are confident, we feel at ease, relaxed, and focused. It is something that we just know; however, we usually only notice when we are *not* confident. When we are not confident, we have more thoughts and doubts, and we are definitely not as comfortable.

- **Confidence is knowing that you're ready**

  Confidence is *not* thinking that you are ready. A question that may help us assess our level of confidence is the following: how would you play if you couldn't fail? The mindset of approaching competition this way is important as long as it doesn't affect the game plan or strategy. For example, throwing a football into triple coverage seems confident, but the game plan suggests idiocy.

- **Confidence is patience**

  Confident athletes never seem to panic or stress when results aren't going their way. We are all going to have bouts of struggle, and we need to remain patient. We need to have confidence in the aspects we can control. We need to trust our preparation, our coaches, our game plans, our emotional management, our routines, and our processes of execution. If we have confidence in the aspects we can control, then we will eventually have good outcomes.

The following are the five paths to confidence. Each section explains the characteristic, discusses how to enhance it, and articulates the ways we can practice becoming more confident.

- Past performances
- Physiological states
- Imagery
- Modeling
- Verbal persuasion

Past Performances
-I've done it before. -

Let's examine two similar scenarios with completely different contexts. The scenario is that we break par, shooting one under; however, in one case, we played in a tournament with good competition on a tough course. In the second scenario, our score was a casual round on our home course with a friend whom we normally beat. While the following examples may have been similar in terms of the execution of shots and scores, the setting, the surrounding circumstances, and the level of competition all have a significant impact on our level of self-efficacy. [29] Similarly, professional golfers often remark that though they are playing well and shooting low scores, they still need to do it in a tournament before they actually "believe it."

The *way we remember our experiences* determines our level of self-efficacy. Thus, there is a crucial need to properly reinforce our memories. We often fail to recall our positive experiences, but in order to gain confidence, we must hold onto our successes.

Because there is so much defeat inherent in the game, the longer we play and the better we become, the more we are inundated with poor memories—the three-putts, the duffed chips, bad tee shots, among others.

We Are Our Memories
-The Future Is Now-

Most of us can recall exactly where we were on the tragic morning of Sept 11th, 2001, but how many of us can remember the morning of Sept 8th? The reason is because our memories are interlinked with our emotions. Rarely, can we recall average events, because these moments are not filled with any emotion. The memories that readily come to mind are ones that are unusual or dramatic.

Think for a second about the last time that you accidentally walked in on someone using a public bathroom. This shocking memory easily surfaces because not only was it filled with emotion (e.g., embarrassment, humor), but also because it was not an average occurrence. Unless you make it common practice, walking in on someone using the bathroom just does not often occur. On the other hand, it is much more difficult to recall a normal occurrence of a time you merely used a public bathroom. To elaborate, we also can't readily recall the "almost" incidents of our lives. The time when we *almost* got pulled over or *almost* got in an accident; however, a fender bender or the time we got pulled over and were late to an important meeting are readily available in our minds.

It is rare that we reflect on our "average" performances. In fact, we may even make it worse by recalling the bad moments that "made it" average as opposed to the instances that "kept it" average. Obviously, leaving shots out on the course is not ideal, but we still must "force" ourselves to remember the good instances of our play. We *try* to focus on the positives of our play and *try* to avoid feeling a lack of confidence from poor executions; however, the problem is that we just don't recall our memories often or correctly.

Quick—think about one shot from your last round. Most of us can more easily think of a poor shot rather than a good one, illustrating the point that we have poor memories. Also, perhaps we recalled one of the latter shots as opposed to one in the middle of the round. It takes more conscious energy to recall shots in the middle of our rounds, because our memories are also strongly influenced by how events finish. Now, if you are the type that recalled a good shot, I bet that one of the shots was the "great" birdie or par saves on hole sixteen, seventeen, or eighteen. If you recalled a poor shot, then perhaps you remembered the "awful" bogey on those same holes. Either way, our memories are often linked to how events end.

Because we all suffer from unproductive thinking sometimes and because positive thinking takes time to develop, another avenue is to properly reflect on the positive aspects from our play. The premise is that there is always at least one part of our game that we liked, and we must choose to *hold onto our successes*. Whether it was a crucial putt for birdie, a good up and down, a good stretch of holes, or overall ball striking, there is *always* at least one positive event from the round.

Learning Experiences Suck!
*"People don't realize how often you have to come in second
in order to finish first."*
—Jack Nicklaus

Tom Lehman has had a long and distinguished career on the PGA Tour, but despite his longevity and victory in the 1996 British Open, he has (only) won five times on tour. The cumulative percentage of his victories per tournaments is barely 1 percent. Kenny Perry has won thirteen PGA Tour events in over nineteen years, which accounts for about 2 percent overall. Arnold Palmer won sixty-two tournaments over his nineteen year PGA career for a winning percentage of 8 percent. For comparison, Tiger Wood's PGA winning percentage is obviously the highest at approximately 27 percent. These stats exemplify that everyone loses much more than he or she wins.

When we shoot a high number, leave shots out there, or miss a short putt to lose the match, it is no fun. Although, it's not supposed to be fun, it is supposed to teach us a lesson. We *actually* learned from the negative experience more so than if we had played really well. However, we did not get what we wanted, which was to play well, and since the problem was so painful, we fail to examine what we learned. We avoid learning by dismissing it (sometimes a good thing), taking a break from golf, distracting ourselves, complaining to others, making excuses, or even self-medicating on the nineteenth hole.

When we play poorly, we must be able to reflect on the round either by talking it out with a knowledgeable colleague or by writing out our thoughts and frustrations. The latter is always preferable, because during the times of frustration, we must learn from these experiences and be able to look back and find out the key points (e.g., I slow down too much during important shots; I have negative self-talk during pressure moments). For example, at the 2008 Nationwide Tour event in Columbus, Stephen Gangluff rediscovered that he plays better when talking throughout the round with either his caddy or playing partners about anything other than golf.

Practice: Hold on to Your Successes
"Simple is powerful."
—Anonymous

Lorena Ochoa experienced the nadir of golf during the 2005 U.S. Open. While she was leading the tournament, she basically drop-kicked the ball on the seventy-second hole into the water to lose the lead and the tournament. It was a horrible experience, yet when she was asked about how she accomplished a positive frame of mind, she stated, "I remember only the good shots. The others—they disappear." [30]

Dr. Joe Whitney and Dr. Craig Wrisberg are the Sport Psychology consultants at the University of Tennessee. One concept that they teach is for athletes to properly remember their performances. They outfit athletes with a journal and instruct them to keep detailed records of their play. After every competition, athletes are instructed to write down two important facets: (1) what did they like and (2) what did they learn.

After successful performances, writing in the journal is pleasant. When we play well, there are tons of examples of what we enjoyed (e.g., I liked playing well, making birdies, getting up and down on sixteen). We can relish our play in our thoughts and create positive memories for ourselves. The more often we play well and reinforce these good thoughts, the more apt we are to stay positive with ourselves.

Golfers must reinforce the good memories. Write down what we liked and what we learned from each competitive round or practice. What may appear "average" at the time could evolve into a database of extremely good memories so that three weeks, six months, and a year down the road, you can gain confidence from replaying these moments. Simply put, golf is hard enough with the inherent difficulties (see *Golf Is Difficult*) that it becomes almost unbearable with a negative state of mind. Create good memories by writing out the details (situation, shot, thoughts or lack thereof, outcome) of one perfect shot each round. Establish these good memories so when you stand over an upcoming shot in the future, your mind will properly think about the last time you hit a perfect shot.

Practice: Check-In Time
-What do you do when you play well?-

Coach Mark Guhne of the University of Tennessee-Chattanooga (UTC) is a three-time Southern Conference coach of the year. During this three-year span, his players won ten collegiate tournaments and held a number one NCAA ranking. Coach Guhne stresses the importance of journaling and recording our thoughts.

His players keep a yardage book at every practice, and whether they are on the range or playing an actual round, they are instructed to rate their commitment for each shot from one to ten. Apart from the outcome of the shot, they also are asked to write out their thoughts and feelings of each shot. The players could write out sentences like, "I was thinking about not missing" or "I committed to the routine." Coach Guhne is resolute that they must learn to battle through negative thoughts and focus on the shot at hand.

Coach Jamie Green of Duke University also stresses the importance of journaling. His players write out their thoughts and feelings at all times during specific practices. He refers to it as a "check in and check out" period, and he is adamant that they write in their journal when they are playing especially well. He wants his players to describe the details when things are going well: What did the course look like? What do I look like? What am I feeling? What are my thoughts?

Physiological States

"I park my car and know I am shooting four under par."
—Lee Trevino

There is a level of physiological activation with any activity ranging from a hundred-meter sprint (high) or sleeping (low). In golf, there are few situations that spark immediate high physical activation, which is why we recognize whether we "feel" confident or not. Moderate levels of physiological arousal are important to playing well, because it stimulates concentration. For instance, think of the last time you were in a car accident (hopefully with minimal damage). These moments of surreal clarity and slow motion are interlinked with our physiological states. The role of physiological states and "feeling" is a crucial link to confidence.

Body Language Doesn't Talk, It Screams.
-What is the feeling of what we want?-

Tim Mack won the gold medal in the pole vault at the 2004 Olympics and indirectly taught a baseball team in Tennessee about the power of body language. Pole-vaulters know and feel success immediately after they clear the bar and their reaction clearly conveys this. Mack's reaction was a powerful two-handed underhanded fist pump that sent excitement through anyone watching. From the moment he would clear the bar and land on the mat, he would "feel" success.

Thus, the nationally ranked baseball team in Farragut, Tennessee, adopted Mack's fist pump. They knew that sliding into or, hopefully, walking into second base was their way of clearing the bar and of briefly savoring that "feeling." Their fist pump was meant to ingrain the feeling that they wanted into their mentality. They would watch the video of

Mack's gold medal performance and emulate the double-handed fist pump and call it the "Tim Mack."

The *fist pump* can also be easily viewed in tennis. Tennis is a great sport because of the competition and the many shifts in momentum from two equally matched players. It also provides us with insight into how we should react. Watch the very best professional players, and you'll find that even *they* celebrate their successful shots with a pump of the fist.

Body language does not talk, it screams. Body language is so important, because it dictates thoughts. Poor body language equals poor thinking, but confident body language equals confident thoughts. We can see golfers who are struggling; their shoulders slump, and their eyes look down. There is no pep in their walk, and most often people become quiet.

Body language is crucial to the importance of celebrating our successes. Our physiological states are intertwined with the feelings that we want to achieve. The more often we celebrate our successes, the more strongly those feelings are cemented.

Practice: Body Language
"He who stops being better, stops being good."
—Oliver Cromwell

What is the feeling that we want to achieve? Dave Pelz and Greg Norman stress the importance of holding the follow-through with the putter. Phil Mickleson always clenches his fist with a pump after a putt drops. Ernie Els tosses away his ball after making birdie. One foursome of amateurs would toss the ball to everyone in the group of whoever made a birdie, which was their way of creating a positive post-shot routine.

Holding the follow-through, pumping a fist, and standing as tall as possible are all easy examples of consistent, positive body language. Good thoughts should accompany good shots so hold onto your success by reminding yourself that you just had a good shot!

This is difficult for many, because we think "that's what we are supposed to do." However, we should be our own best friend on the course by reminding ourselves of a "good follow-through", "nice roll", or "good shot."

Imagery

"I'm practicing winning."
—Scott Stallings

Billy Mills won the ten-thousand-meter gold medal in 1964 in Tokyo. He was the consummate underdog, so much so that when the U.S. team provided their runners with new shoes, he was not even given a pair. He was told, "We only have shoes for those expected to medal." Even after he miraculously won, a Japanese reporter asked him, "Who are you?" To Mills, it did not matter that he was unknown or that he was competing against the world record holder, Ron Clarke, or that Clarke's best time was almost a minute faster than his own.

Mills was far ahead of his time when it came to the manner in which he finished his practices. He used to complete every practice by sprinting a hundred meters while he imagined winning the ten-thousand-meter gold. He imagined that he was a "breath of wind," and he would picture himself running past Clarke for the win. The race was one of the greatest upsets of all time, yet the fashion in which he won the race was inspiring and frankly eerie at the same time. Mills won the ten-thousand-meter gold medal in 1964 in exactly the same fashion as he used to finish his practices (watch the finish at billymills.org).

Imagery is the most powerful tool any athlete can utilize. It is the process of creating or recreating experiences in the mind. [31] Simply put, the best athletes mentally prepare through imagery. On the range at a PGA event this past year, I approached a player and asked what he was working on. He replied that he was picturing the shots he would hit with the wind in his face on the back nine.

Prior to the 2004 Olympic trials, Michael Phelps stated, "Before the [Olympic] trials, I was doing a lot of relaxing exercises and visualization. And I think that that helped me to get a feel of what it was gonna be like when I got there." [32] Jack Nicklaus repeatedly stated, "I never hit a shot, not even in practice, without having a very sharp, in-focus picture of it in my head." Both of these examples are important not only because of the source, but they utilized imagery in practice as well.

First, we must examine why people *do not* utilize imagery. The inability to accurately control images sometimes causes us to see ourselves performing exactly how we do not want to. It doesn't take long for someone to give up on imagery if he or she always sees himself or herself missing the putt or hitting it into a watery grave. In addition, if we only try to picture or feel the shot during competition, then we are changing our routine and possibly adding a distraction, which may hinder our performance. As a result, we then become hesitant to use imagery and convince ourselves that it is a waste of time and effort. The second reason why people are hesitant to use imagery is the misconception surrounding the entire process. Oftentimes people think that it is similar to using hypnosis or listening to subliminal tapes, only used while lying down in bed.

Most of us have (and still do) used imagery at some point, but we just may be unaware of our use. If we have imagined a five-footer for the U.S. Open, pictured a tough shot on the range, or visualized a lake in front of us that isn't there, then we have used imagery. The essence of imagery is to harness its effectiveness for constant use in our games. The type of imagery suggested below can be used during practice and should become a complement to the pre-shot routine. Once imagery becomes a staple of the pre-shot routine, it can eventually be used in competition. It is the surest and most powerful way to enhance performance.

Practice: Imagery
"I fear not the man who has practiced 10,000 kicks once, but the man who has practiced one kick 10,000 times."
—*Bruce Lee*

Each of us has a dominant style of imagery. We either (1) picture the shot *or* (2) picture the target. Strictly speaking, they are not mutually exclusive; meaning that we can accomplish both, but because we have a dominant style, it is important to only utilize one, or else the process could become cumbersome.

We must become proficient and master either (1) picturing the shot *or* (2) picturing the target as opposed to trying to tinker with different styles or rarely employing it. It must become part of the pre-shot routine and mastered during practice.

Picturing the shot:

By picturing the shot, we should be able to more easily trace the ball flight in our mind, seeing it arch and land. Because there are often shots that do not appeal to our "eye," it directly impacts our mind and causes us to hit the shot that we have just imagined. For example, you may play a shot over a bunker either on a chip shot or a par-three. If we have utilized imagery in practice, then we should be able see the ball come off the club face, land, and roll exactly how we have pictured.

Putting is the platform in which some of us more naturally picture the shot. We actually see the line that the ball will take and how the ball will enter the cup. During this process, it is easy to become lazy and "kind of" see the ball on the line. It is important to picture the entire putt, especially the last few feet, and really emphasize seeing where the ball will enter the cup.

Picturing the target:

Jackie Burke won sixteen PGA events in his career, including the 1956 Masters and the PGA Tour championship. He exclusively used aerial targets such as clouds or tree tops far in the distance as the smallest possible targets.

Contrary to seeing the ball flight, some of us may more naturally picture the target. In this, we *feel* the swing needed to get the ball to the target. Seeing the entire shot does not necessarily appeal to all, whereas having a target pictured might. It is important that we visualize the smallest possible target for the ball's landing. Similarly in putting, if we more easily picture the target, then drawing a line may be too much information. We putt more effectively when we pick a spot (e.g., two inches outside, right lip, back of the cup) and hold the target in our minds as we stroke the ball.

Modeling

-I've seen it done, so I know I can do it.-

Personally, I always seem to play better golf after I return from caddying a professional tournament. It makes sense, because I just spent the last week watching the swings and games of the best golfers in the world.

Modeling (i.e., vicarious experience) is one of the primary ways that we actually learn a specific behavior. Watch any infant learn any behavior or language, and you'll notice that the infant's new habits have been modeled after his or her parents. Modeling is how we learn to brush our teeth, rebound a basketball, drive a car, or practice table manners. In essence, one of the ways we can know that we gain confidence is through the observation of others.

The Human Highlight
-We are our own best model.-

Dominque Wilkins was a nine-time NBA all-star and hall of famer, but he was mostly known for his dunks. Arguably the best dunker in the game, he would "perform" his windmill dunks during actual games. His moniker came to be known as the "Human Highlight Film" for his high-flying antics and the way that he threw the ball down. Anyone can still check out his performances via the large collection of video highlights.

Prior to winning the 2009 Masters, Angel Cabrera doubted his own putting, so his coach, Mike Epps, brought along a highlight reel of Angel winning the U.S. Open at Oakmont. He showed the edited video of him sinking a ten-foot birdie on the seventeenth hole and saving par with a six-footer on the playoff hole. "He is always telling me how many putts he doesn't make," coach Epps stated. "I tell [sic] him, 'Hey, just watch this.'"
33

We can become our own best model, and using video highlights of our own performances reinforces our strengths and serves as an example of self-modeling. Self-modeling makes the unobservable observable. Research has shown that watching ourselves do something makes us believe it can be accomplished.

Self-modeling has been used as an intervention strategy with children who suffer from stuttering disorders. [34] Unfortunately, stuttering has negative implications, especially for school-age individuals, which can hinder one's social development and overall confidence. Bray's research examined the effects on individuals who watched themselves speaking on edited versions of videotape that removed all the instances of stuttering. Participants were shown five-minute videotapes of themselves speaking fluently. After seven occasions of watching themselves speak without stuttering, all showed a decrease in stuttering behavior. The successes of the treatments were a result of self-modeling and developing a belief that they could speak fluently. It is difficult to argue with the previous superior performances of ourselves after all.

Bear witness and savor our past successes as opposed to becoming mired in our past failures. Conjuring up positive images becomes more common the more often we witness our own past successes, and this provides a base to visualize these aspects instead of the negative images or thoughts. Because negative thinking accompanies struggles with confidence, quality video highlights serve as a means for countering these negative thoughts.

Most video, however, is only used as a means of skill development and analysis of the swing. There isn't anything inherently wrong with viewing faults of the swing, yet over time, it reinforces a "golf swing" mentality and engrosses the player with mechanics of the swing, which could ultimately distract one from focusing on the target. Vijay Singh is renowned for his aversion to using video for his swing. "I don't like working with videos [of the swing], because you see so many different things … Then you try to make the swing look pretty instead of effective." [35]

Practice: Human Highlight
-Seeing is believing-

One key to building or repairing self-confidence is to create our own human highlight film. The highlights on ESPN usually don't show the mistakes or average plays from a game unless they were significant to the outcome. A running back may rush for well over a hundred yards, but these instances of four- or five-yard runs blend into the fray (although crucial for success). To create a proper highlight film, edit particular, positive clips, and even introduce a particular theme of music to specific parts of the highlight film.

Verbal Persuasion

"Yes, you can!"
—Any Coach

Gary Player would only listen to certain people around him. If anyone in his presence started to talk negatively about golf, he would just walk away. What a skill, considering the amount of negative talk after a round in the clubhouse or on the range. This was a top player who understood the importance of listening and ignoring and wanted no part of the misery speak of most other golfers.

Off the course, there are many voices that we can either choose to listen to or not. Logically, the number of voices that we choose to listen to is an indicator of our level of confidence. Mike Mussina of the Yankees asked five different coaches, including Joe Torre, why he was struggling during the 2007 season. Unfortunately, he received five different answers, all of them correct. Thus, he concluded, "I just had to go out there and go with what I had and believe it was good enough." [25] Other people's voices can have a tremendous impact, and it is imperative that we choose wisely when we determine to which voices we want to listen.

Some voices may try to instruct, motivate, and educate, while others, unfortunately, may (intentionally or unintentionally) make us feel hurt, guilty, or unconfident. For example, during the 2007 Super Bowl run, Colts president Bill Polian continually preached to listen to "one voice." He explained, "It's important that the players not get distracted by those other voices, of which there are so many, and just concentrate on the task at hand. Just listen to the voice that can show them how to succeed, and that voice is (Coach Tony Dungy's)." [36]

The Voice(s)
-Who are we listening to?-

Joe Simpson was an expert climber, but he fell down a hundred-foot crevasse, broke his leg, and waited alone in the snowy Andes Mountains. He suffered from severe dehydration and frostbite, and he knew he still had a long solo journey ahead of him if he wanted to reach safety. In his book, *Touching the Void*, he describes how he could hear two voices. One voice would daydream, ramble disconnected thoughts, and sing song lyrics, while the other one would rationalize, so he labeled it "the voice."

As he remarkably traversed the mountain for three days by hopping on one leg to his original base camp, it was "the voice" that saved him. The voice was essentially his savior, and it would tell him "what to do" and "how to do it." "*Get moving … Don't lie there … Get going … There are things to be done … Don't think about it … Just do it.*"[37] However, the voice wouldn't always be cooperative and would sometimes tell him to lie down. Joe Simpson's experience illustrates that we all have two voices—the "other" voice and "the voice"—and we must constantly choose which voice we want to follow.

The "other" voice may tell us that 6:00 am is too early to train, but "the voice" may tell us to get up and do it. The "other" voice may try to remind us about all the bad shots we have been hitting. The "other" voice may tell us that we are not quite good enough, that we have too many weaknesses, or that we just don't have the talent. The "other" voice tries to make us lose focus, make excuses, and feel weak. The "other" voice often makes us question our commitment, our goals, and sometimes our coaches. The "other" voice does not push us to become better, seek help, or practice smarter.

Vince Lombardi's premise that "fatigue makes cowards of us all" is very apparent. The "other" voice does not show up when things are going well. It only shows up during times of doubt, weakness, or fatigue—the times when we are most apt to actually listen. The "other" voice will show up when we are trying to post a score or when we start to make tentative or bad swings.

All of us have this "other" voice, even the best tennis player. For instance, Roger Federer, a man who called his 2006 U.S. Open quarter-final against James Blake the toughest test of the two weeks, stated:

> *I get doubts once in a while, and early on in the tournament, they're always there. But it doesn't mean I'm going to play bad. It's just, like, all of a sudden, you have these five minutes where you think, and 'Maybe I'm not going to win this thing.' Because maybe I just don't feel quite right or maybe the other guys are playing very well. It's just about turning that corner at the right moment and telling yourself, 'Well, I think you can do it again.' And that's what I did.* [38]

Merely having the "other" voice does not mean that bad things are going to happen, but we have to train the mind not to listen. If we succumb to the "other" voice, we forfeit our competitiveness and quit either mentally or physically. Lance Armstrong also experiences the "other" voice and discusses not listening to the pain. He has said, "Pain is temporary. It may last a minute, or an hour, or a day, or a year, but eventually it will subside and something else will take its place. If I quit, however, it lasts forever." [39]

Mental toughness training demands that we properly train the voice. Across all sports with physical pain (swimming, running, football), "the voice" will emerge in practice with thoughts and questions like the following: How many more sets? Will I make it? Why do I feel so awful? In golf however, "the voice" often does not even materialize in practice. If it does, it is usually structured around the swing, perhaps saying the following: Stay out in front. Stay behind the ball. Fire through it. More than likely, the voice usually only shows up during actual play and asks questions that we can't answer at the time: Why can't I play today? Why do I even play? Will I even break par?

The disparity in other sports is that "the voice" is actually trained during practice to be effective during competition, whereas the opposite is true for golf. Competitive rounds of golf are the times when "the voice" appears, and becoming mentally tough requires that we train the voice during practice to help us in competition.

Needing, Wanting, & Justing
"People need to be reminded, more often than they need to be instructed."
—Samuel Johnson

A fox is walking in the forest and sees some grapes high in the trees. The fox says, "I bet those are the sweetest grapes ever." The fox tries jumping as high as possible to reach the grapes, but he cannot get them. So, the fox then says, "I bet those grapes really aren't that sweet." Except just as he quits trying, a bird accidently knocks off some grapes, and the fox devours them. To the fox's surprise, they are indeed the sweetest grapes ever. So, the fox tries again to jump and reach the remaining grapes on the tree and again the fox can't reach them. Thus, the fox states, "I bet I had the last good grapes on the tree."[40]

The moral of the above fable is that we can't hold two beliefs at once. We must choose what to believe and how to act according to our beliefs, or it results in "cognitive dissonance." Cognitive dissonance is the mental discomfort caused by simultaneously holding two contradictory beliefs. For example, try rooting for the opposing team during a football game, and you'll experience it firsthand. The problem is that we contribute to this cognitive dissonance through the voice in practice and competition.

Oftentimes, while I caddied for professional golfers, there were critical moments with more pressure during the round. During these instances among athletes, there was always increased tension, shorter breaths, and counterproductive over-thinking, which all added undue pressure.

During these important moments, we become very "needy." I "need" this putt, or I "need" to get up and down. Across all sports, athletes and coaches alike add worthless pressure through these thoughts: We "need" this goal. I "need" a big inning. I "need" to throw a strike. Or the worst ever: I "need" a win.

The *moment itself* provides enough excitement, and "needing" it to happen not only adds undue pressure, but contributes to a lack of mental toughness. Let's examine the situation: [In competition] If we need something, then it is safe to assume that we are completely dedicated to achieving this short-term goal; however, if it doesn't turn out as planned, then how can we justify dismissing it and moving on? Cognitive dissonance will occur, and we feel like we're rooting for the opposing team.

The "needing" mindset handicaps our thoughts, places unrealistic expectations on ourselves, and does not allow any flexibility in our mindset. Cutting ourselves some slack will facilitate performance. Thus, it is important to recognize the difference between "wants" and "needs." Notice the difference between statements like "I need to play well" and "I want to play well!" I "would like" this putt. I "would like" to get up and down here. I "want" to play well.

Becoming mentally tough requires us to import these "would like to" words and feelings into our minds as opposed to the "needing it to" statements. Employing these thoughts during practice and play is important during pressure situations. Probably more important is the underlying belief in these thoughts of "wanting, not needing." It is *you* who must decide whether or not you need events to happen to be a worthwhile person.

Our perception of the situation is the cause of pressure; however, there is a time and place to discuss perspective. We can tell ourselves that we *really, really, really "want"* this putt as opposed to stating that we *really, really "need"* this putt, but it seems to produce the same result of adding undue pressure.

Another strategy during competition and practice is to effectively train the voice that will prevent undue pressure. One technique is to "just." It allows some freedom to complete the task, because it is not termed in absolutes:

- "Just" start it online

- "Just" put a good swing on it

- "Just" stay aggressive

- "Just" put it here

When pressure mounts, it is crucial to allow yourself some room to think effectively, and using the word "just" provides a clear goal.

The Post-Shot Routine

*"The more you see yourself as what you'd like to become, and act as if
what you want is already there, the more you'll activate those dormant
forces that will collaborate to transform your dream into your reality."*
—Wayne Dyer

Momentum is like pancakes. Pancakes can be ordered in a variety of
ways (silver dollar, regular, buttermilk) and are even named differently
(i.e., flapjacks, hotcakes) depending on where you are regionally. Entire
restaurants are even named after this morning delicacy—International
House of Pancakes. Pancakes, though, usually consist of more than just
one. One pancake seems to go against all we know about the dish.

Momentum is very similar to pancakes in this regard. One event does
not cause us to become angry or lose our focus. It is a stack of these events
combined that cause frustration. If we look back at a round, it is usually
the culmination of events that instill anger in us—the fat shot on hole
four, the pushed drive on hole seven, the power-lip out on hole twelve,
the bad bounce into the bunker on hole fourteen. Any of these considered
separately are "just part of the game"; however, when they are stacked upon
one another, these events resemble pancakes, and together cause a lack of
momentum. A string of birdies, par saves, or a clutch putt can also produce
good feelings, and riding the wave of positive momentum is much easier
than trying to stem the tide of negative momentum.

Developing a post-shot routine is usually the missing link to a good
pre-shot routine. After the shot? Absolutely! Mental toughness requires a
good response to performance, because it impacts the approach.

A bad shot (e.g., a missed putt, a three-putt, a poor chip) followed by
a bad response is likely to produce a bad pre-shot routine, which produces
a negative cycle. (See the figure below for how the cycle works.) If the
response is forfeited, the approach will suffer, and performance will then
suffer.

Missed Birdie → So What!

3-putt   or

Poor chip   Now What?

Good or Bad

Pre-shot routine

The way to incorporate a good response into your game is to develop and maintain a post-shot routine. Establishing a post-shot routine does not mean that you should act like a robot devoid of emotion. A post-shot routine simply means incorporating specific thoughts and body language to ensure a quality next shot.

So What? Or Now What?
"Character is destiny."
—Heraclitus

What are the words that we say to ourselves after a good or poor shot? The context of these powerful words is almost as important as the message they convey. "So what" means that everything is still okay and no damage has been done, but it also means more than mere reassurance.

"So what" is a reminder that we have to re-focus. The context of these words is also crucial because holding on to a bad play does not allow anyone an opportunity to achieve his or her best. U.S. Navy SEAL training also utilizes the phrase of "so what." "Instructors would routinely say 'so what' if one of the SEALs was complaining of being in the ocean for twenty-four straight hours, undergoing intense training that is almost unbearable." [41]

Of course, without properly training our mind in practice, we naturally assume a "now what" mentality. "Now what" is a non-directed, rhetorical question, and it is similar to throwing up our hands in disbelief or waving the white flag of surrender. When we say things to ourselves sarcastically like "that's great," it essentially means "now what?"

Practice: The Voice
-Our own faults, rarely appear to ourselves.-

Along with our physical practice, we must practice recognizing the types of thoughts that help and hurt our performance. This type of practice needs to be continually monitored on the "front end," for listening to the "other" voices too long makes it even more difficult to actually realize what we are saying to ourselves.

Good Thoughts
-Good thoughts-

Tommy Pharr, future hall of fame baseball coach in Tennessee, continually shouts the following statement to his players: "Good thoughts." Essentially, this instruction is a reminder to merely have good thoughts going into a pressure situation. For instance, stepping up to the plate with bases loaded and two outs on the board just is not a time to focus on what could go wrong, so he would say, "Good thoughts." Often as a caddy, I use this reminder during some important moments when I realize my golfer is having some doubts about the shot. It serves as a reminder to focus on what we are trying to do and not on the possible repercussions of a bad shot. Of course, having a coach or caddy remind us is always helpful, but we have to be our own coach and train our voice to think of good thoughts, too.

What are some other strategies we can use to help us develop good thoughts and focus on the task at hand? Fred Couples, 1992 Masters champion, is considered to have one of the prettiest swings in golf and one of the most relaxed mentalities; however, Davis Love III stated, "He is more tense on the golf course than he is anywhere." Couples used a specific technique whenever he encountered pressure moments on the golf course.

He repeated the following to help relax: "It's no big deal. It's no big deal. It's no big deal."

One aspect to help focus is to develop a *mantra*. This mantra should be short, personal, and designed as a cue to re-focus. For instance, Hank Aaron's mantra was "keep swinging," and the 2006 Rutgers football team developed a mantra of "keep chopping wood." Another mantra could be WIN (What's important now?). Or it could be a simple reminder to "relax."

Often it is not the ability to focus but rather the ability to refocus. When thoughts or outside distractions interfere with our focus, it is the ability to *refocus* that is important. We should develop an effective mantra for both poor and quality shots. The importance is to *refocus after a poor shot* and *after a good shot*. The ability to focus and re-focus during competition is a skill that can be strengthened through quality practice.

Develop your poor shot mantra:

Keeping momentum going depends on maximizing the small successes; however, there is a tendency to put too much pressure on oneself instead of "just" executing the shot. Because we have time on our side between shots, we should also develop our mantra for what we will say to ourselves after a quality shot.

Develop your good shot mantra:

Mentally Tough Putting

"Putting is more mental than it is physical."
—Dave Stockton

The toughest putt in all of golf occurs during the final hole during the final stage of Q-school. Ted Purdy was faced with the exact situation at the 2008 Q-school finals. He had played well all week, and at the end of the six days, he "had" to make a ten-footer to finish in eighteenth place and secure his 2009 PGA card.

There was more to this putt than anyone "just" needing to make it. Ted Purdy was simply not a good putter, and his putting average for the past few years was poor at best. He was ranked 191st on tour in 2008, 177th in 2007, and 144th in 2006. Thus, as his putting coach Pat O'Brien commented, "There was a lot of garbage in the head about being a bad putter."

How do you become a mentally tough putter when the results have convinced you that you are a bad putter? Pat O'Brien is also the putting coach for Zach Johnson and Vaughn Taylor. Before Q-school, Ted Purdy and he returned to perfecting his mechanics that helped lead to Ted making the final putt. Coach O'Brien feels that one's mechanics must first be fundamentally perfect (e.g., posture, alignment, structure, and ball position).

The mechanics of the putting stroke begin (and end) with correct fundamentals. The posture, grip, ball position, alignment, stroke, and follow-through must be fundamentally sound. If these are inconsistent, then we will ultimately return to addressing fundamentals in practice. When faced in a situation of a "must-make" putt, we cannot second-guess if our fundamentals are correct.

Before he became the head golf coach at Duke University, Jamie Green was the head coach at UNC Charlotte for six years, held a number one team ranking and two top ten NCAA finishes, and was voted Atlantic-10 Conference coach of the year three times.

Coach Green has stated that evaluating our own putting can become too emotional and personal. So he challenged his players to run through a two-step checklist to diagnose the cause of poor putts. We should first assess mechanics; (1) did we make a solid stroke and start the putt on line? If we incorrectly hit a few putts during the round, then we can quickly deduce that the stroke is off and later return to perfecting mechanics.

One way to assess mechanics is to make certain that our alignment with their line is correct. It is necessary to periodically check that the line and stroke is correct and often using putting aids can really assist:

- **Alignment tools**-especially by EyeLine® golf can really enhance and reinforce proper putting alignment.

- **Chalk lines**-are intended to take reading the putt out of the equation and again reinforce one's alignment.

- **Playing partners and teaching professionals**-can help by having them look at how the ball is coming off the putter face and if it is on the correct path.

Practice: Commit to the Line
"I have kept the faith."
—Timothy 4:7

Pat Sellers, a Rife Putters' representative, has spoken with, watched, outfitted, and played with some of the greatest golfers in the history of the game. His years of applied experience on the PGA Tour led him to undertake a project that allowed him to interview the game's best putters. Pat Sellers' interviews revealed that *confidence* was the key to successful putting and that the best putters knew their line was correct. As a result, no thoughts or doubts entered their minds. Not surprisingly, none of the greatest putters stated mechanical aspects were the key to success on the moss.

In order to become a great putter, you must commit to the line! Unfortunately, how many times have we second-guessed or doubted the line while we were standing over the putt? These are awful times, because more often than not, we miss the putt and become upset. More importantly, we are upset at ourselves for doubting the line, too. These instances are very difficult and require more mental energy than necessary.

We must commit to the line of the putt behind the ball. Picking the line behind the ball ensures that you are confident about the line you've chosen. If at any time you doubt the line, then you must start the entire routine over again.

We should also make certain that our alignment with our target is also correct. Pat Sellers cites the fact that current pros that switch putters often encounter alignment issues because of the different visual putter face. Tommy "Two Gloves" Gainey discovered his alignment issues firsthand when he was aiming left of the target. Pat Sellers outfitted him with the correct putter for his alignment, and he proceeded to make four out of the next six cuts, which culminated in a second place finish ($496,800) at the last event of the 2008 season. [42]

Pre-putt Routine
-How important is it?-

Jim Furyk and Aaron Baddley are two great putters who vary greatly in the timing of their putting routines; however, these players are consistent in their behaviors and timing of their routines. Their timing rarely varies when they play. In fact, Aaron Baddley's superfast routine of reading the line and stroking the putt has never varied since he was an amateur. On the other hand, Jim Furyk takes a long time lining up the putt. He stands over it and lines it up again before he hits. In fact, the major deviation in Jim Furyk's routine during the 2006 U.S. Open at Winged Foot on the seventy-second hole may have caused him to miss the putt. Jim Furyk took much longer than his already deliberate routine, and unfortunately, he missed the par putt to finish second.

Do faster putting routines equate to improved accuracy, or do players who take longer on their routines make more putts? We examined the timing of putting routines in collegiate golfers and the correlation with success. We examined at two fifty-four-hole collegiate golf tournaments.

The first tournament revealed that during made putts, pre-putt routines were significantly shorter in duration. When golfers made the putt, the average time was 21.9 seconds. However, when golfers missed the putt, the mean time was 27.33 seconds.

However, because putting routines are player-specific, a player can still be just as successful no matter whether he or she takes longer or shorter pre-putt routines. Our research found that consistency of time was the most important factor and significantly related to the probability of players making the putt. [43]

Because putting is a self-paced task and the near-expert level of the collegiate golfers yielded established and near "automatic" pre-shot routines, results of this putting study along with others suggest that the consistency of pre-putt routines produce fewer thoughts, which results in more consistent behaviors and outcomes. [44, 45]

Hence, fewer thoughts during the pre-putt routine seems to equal less time, which suggests the player trusts his or her line and stroke. But the more we deviate from our own routine, the more chances favor poor thinking and trying to steer the putt.

On the Clock

"You can slow down a race-horse easier than you can speed up a turtle."
—Barry Shular

Because there are two waves of golfers (morning and afternoon tee times) at every PGA tournament, keeping pace is crucial. Pace can trickle down, and everyone can become affected by slow play. Thus, there are PGA officials strategically placed around the course in case players need a ruling, but they also help keep the pace of play by sneaking out from the bushes in their carts and announcing that the entire group is "on the clock." From that moment on, each player is timed by the official from reaching his or her ball through the execution of the shot. Hall of fame PGA member Don Essig III, has served as a top PGA rules official since 1964. He has officiated over major championships, won the 1957 U.S. Amateur Public Links Championship, and played professionally alongside Arnold Palmer and Jack Nicklaus. Being a master teaching professional, he has stated, "Ninety percent of players improve when they are put on the clock."

Practice: The Mental Clock
"Time's a wastin."
—June Carter

This drill requires that we know our own internal clock while we putt. We should have someone else time it or we can simply count. The timing of your pre-putt routine is important, and it must be the same for every putt, regardless of distance. The clock starts the moment you take the first step toward the ball. 1 … 2 … 3 … 4 … Go through your entire routine, and stop the clock the moment you begin your stroke. 5 … 6 … 7 … 8 … There is not a perfect timing mechanism as it depends on you. 9 … 10 … 11 … 12 … 13 … 14 … For instance, Jim Furyk and Aaron Baddley's routines are worlds apart in time. 15 … 16 … 17 … 18 … 19 … 20 …

Please note though that anything over twenty seconds is considered *very* long, and the longer the count, the more things can go wrong (i.e. doubting the line, thinking about the stroke, thinking about the situation, worrying about the score, etc.).

Practice: Focus on the Clock
"Time will pass; will you?"
—My third grade teacher

The mere concept of counting is profound when given thought. How cool was it when we first counted to ten as a kid? What about when we first counted to ten in Spanish?

During this drill, the actual *counting* of the routine is important, because it fills the mind with an important aspect (pre-putt routine) and it does not allow any other thoughts to enter our mind. If done correctly, the only thought that will occupy our mind is the counting.

This drill takes practice and discipline, because often we may "think" we are counting, but other thoughts are entering our mind without our awareness. When this occurs, we must be disciplined enough to start our routine over. If we continue through the routine when other thoughts enter our mind without starting over, we are going through the "motions" and are no longer focused on the task at hand.

This drill must be situated *on the practice* green. Once our mental clock is determined, only then can it be transferred onto the actual course of play. While this drill is very powerful, it probably takes the most time to ingrain.

Practice: The Phil Parkin
"My practice was more difficult than competition."
—Phil Parkin

Phil Parkin is probably one of the best golfer's who has never become too famous with most fans. He is currently a golf coach, and commentator for *The Golf Channel*. In his playing days, he won the 1983 British Amateur, and was first team All-American at Texas A&M. He routinely beat players like Colin Montgomerie and Davis Love III and even played a collegiate tournament only with irons just to see how well he would do (second place). Unfortunately, immediately after he turned professional in 1984, he developed a debilitating eye condition that affected his entire depth perception and rendered his green-reading skills entirely useless. He stated, "I wish I would have had just a few years as a professional with good eyes."

His putting drill would sometimes take him hours to complete, but he always remained until it was done. The drill was to two-putt every hole on the green three times each. If a ball was three-putted anywhere, he would start the drill over.

During this drill, he would place three balls on one spot on the edge of the green and would have to two-putt each ball to every single hole. Depending on the number of holes on the green, there could be forty-footers or twenty-footers with various slopes throughout. Phil stated that he was always nervous coming to the last hole, thinking about how he had to two-putt it three times in a row. Anything in a tournament didn't compare.

Practice: The Bernhard Langer
"So when I was told to work ten or twelve hours a day, as an assistant
pro, I didn't complain."
—Bernhard Langer

Regrettably, people only remember Bernhard Langer's experience with the yips and forget that during his prime he was a great putter. He used to practice holing his putts in a variety of speeds: straight in, falling in from the left, and falling in from the right. This drill is to practice holing putts with three different speeds. There are various ways to make short putts, so we should know whether we are a firm putter or one that likes to die the ball in the hole. Set up three four-foot putts and

- Make three in a row that "just" drop in the cup

- Hole three in a row that slam in the back of the cup

- Make three putts in a row with normal speed

This drill will reinforce the speed of the putts you want by acclimating you to different speeds.

Practice: The Phil Mickelson
"Just Do It."
—Nike

This putting drill exemplifies mental toughness. The goal is to *make a hundred consecutive three-footers*. There are a variety of ways to set up this drill (e.g., circle of balls around hole, same spot, etc.). It may help if you have a partner (or caddy) to replace the balls, because getting in a groove and feeling momentum will then happen more often with fewer interruptions.

Notice that this drill is simple, but not easy. It may take a while to finish, but committing to it is a big accomplishment. As a result, it is important to build up to a hundred three-footers. Begin by setting up this drill once per week and making twenty-five or thirty putts in a row. After each practice, increase the number by ten putts. The overall outcome is that during competition when you encounter a short putt, your first thoughts should go back the success with this drill.

Practice: Rhythm Is Gonna Get You
"Success is never final."
—Winston Churchill

The following drill was introduced at a PGA event by Jonathan Fricke, who was one of the best putters on tour. It is a drill designed to create pressure and build confidence, but it also reinforces a proper rhythm and routine.

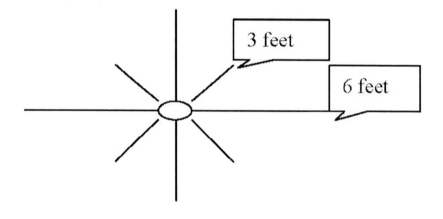

He sets up a square box on the putting green, with four tees at three feet, and four tees at six feet (see image). Next, he creates pressure. He arranges the drill so that he must make ten in a row from three feet at each spot. After he completes the three-footers, he moves back to the six-footers and resumes the drill by making five in a row from each of the four positions.

Second, and more importantly, he reinforces his routine and establishes a consistent rhythm during his putting through this drill. He solidifies his routine and rhythm on the greens by the manner in which he looks at the hole, line, and ball. He stresses the importance of keeping the pace of the stroke exactly the same regardless of the length of the putt. Thus, the only aspect that changes is the length of the stroke. The key for Jonathan Fricke is the manner in which he draws his eyes back to the ball. He establishes a constant rhythm by the speed at which he draws his eyes back to the ball. Putts that are longer result in pulling his eyes back slower so that he can feel the length of the stroke. Putts that are straight or shorter in length are met with drawing his eyes back to the ball a bit quicker. Fricke stated, "I believe no matter what aspect we are working on, we should practice it as consistent as possible, because once we are under the gun, it has to be simple."

Practice: Call Your Shot
"An uncommitted life, is not worth living."
—Marshall Fishwick

Babe Ruth had been mythically credited of calling his shot during the 1932 World Series against the Cubs. He was reportedly "heckled" by the Cubs players, and in the fifth inning of game three, he apparently raised his arm, pointed at the stands, and then hit a homerun, calling his shot. David Morland IV, PGA Tour player and two-time winner on the Nationwide tour, restored his stellar putting by modifying his routine. He returned to a solid routine and a former strategy of "calling his shot." He now aligns himself by extending his arm and pointing at the ball. He raises his arm to point at the hole and points back to the ball. This routine has a goal of both solidifying the correct line of the putt and creating a sense of confidence by calling his shot before he takes the putt.

Practice: Survive and Move On
"Get the ball to the hole."
—Dave Pelz

I witnessed Garret Clegg conduct the following drill on a quiet Monday on the Nationwide Tour. We discussed the influence of UNLV head golf coach Dwaine Knight. Knight is a two-time coach of the year, and his pupils include Adam Scott, Chris Riley, Chad Campbell, and Ryan Moore. His philosophy is similar to another great short-game teacher, Dave Pelz, who preaches "get the ball to the hole." The rationale of emphasizing speed drills is that any short putt has absolutely *no chance* of going in.

However, the trepidation of running the ball past the hole brings into play the dreaded three-putt; there is no other way around it. Three-putting can become so pervasive that it infects our subconscious mind as well. Of course, we don't stand over a putt and think, "Don't three-putt it," but we may stand over makeable putts (eight to fifteen feet) and due to a lack of commitment just lag it close.

The below speed game is meant to instill mental toughness for putting through the emphasis on the proper speed. Along with the other drills throughout this book, it must be completed. The game is designed to not only teach one to judge the correct speed but to deal with feelings of frustration and pressure. The purpose of the speed drill game is similar to NCAA March Madness during tournament time. You must "survive and move on."

Set-Up: (see image)

1. Tees, markers, or a string line should be set up forty inches past the hole that resemble a box. This length should fit a three-foot putt with a few inches of extra room. The ball must *always* be within the confines to count.

2. The first three balls are set up on the same side, the first ball being placed seven feet from the hole and approximately two feet (one step) between each ball. There are *three total rounds*, and there should be three putts on each side for a total of six putts.

Game:

3. The goal is to putt the ball in or past the hole within the confines of the box. The *score must be even or under par* after six putts to continue onto the next round.

4. Scoring is as follows: -1 for a made putt, 0 for a putt past the hole and between the markers, and +1 for any putt short or

past the markers. If the score is above par, then you must start over at round one.

5. After each successful round, the marker on the previous round closest to the hole moves back. Thus, during the last round, the shortest putt is the longest putt from the first round.

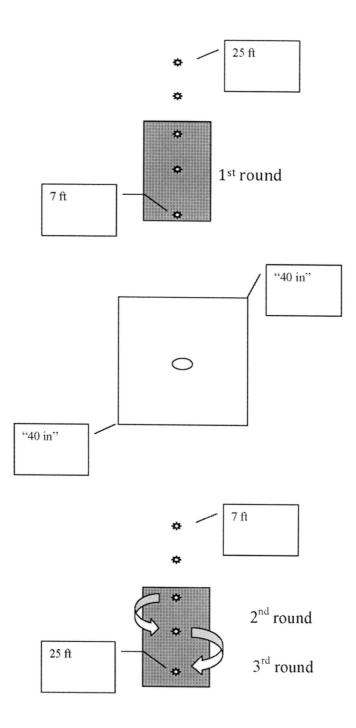

The Don'ts of Mental Toughness

Don't Expect to Win Every Tournament

-A bad dress rehearsal foretells a good opening night.-

Brendan Steele, a player on the Nationwide Tour, had conditional status in 2008, meaning that the number of PGA tournaments he could enter was directly influenced by how well he played (obviously more pressure than one with full status). During one tournament at the Prince Georges Open in Maryland, he was low on the list of alternates, and he was not likely to get into the tournament. Consequently, he flew back home to California on Tuesday to be with his wife, and when he got off the plane, he discovered that he was now entered in the tourney. He returned on a red-eye flight and arrived back in Maryland on Thursday morning for his early afternoon tee time. He had to play the course at the highest level, without seeing it once before, with no sleep and with a local caddy on her very first assignment.

Fortunately, he was able to play well enough to make the cut and actually finished Sunday with one of the only bogey free rounds; but the larger story is how he was able to accomplish this feat. He remarked that there were no expectations as he was not able to "look ahead" to certain holes, and he was only focused on "playing golf."

The power of having no expectations has been illustrated by other professionals. A similar experience occurred with Alex Cejka at the Zurich Classic in New Orleans. Alex thought he had missed the cut and flew back to Las Vegas, but bad weather eliminated the cut line, so he flew to Houston and drove through the night to the tourney. He arrived an hour before his tee time, but his clubs and clothes had not arrived! He played the final round with borrowed clubs and surprisingly played his best round of the week at one under par. Another example of playing with no expectations was Scott Dunlap at the 2000 PGA Championship. He shot an opening round sixty-six despite coming off a bad cold and not playing for a month [46]

In 2002 at the Tampa Bay Classic, K. J. Choi had been suffering from terrible stomach pains. Many saw him grabbing his abdomen during the final round. He later stated that the pain made him say to himself, "I'll just take it hole by hole." He won the tournament by an amazing seven shots and had his appendix removed the next day.[47]

The University of Virginia men's golf team was in sixteenth place during the 2008 regional tournament in which only the top ten teams advanced to the NCAA championships. When UVA arrived in Chattanooga that morning, there was a long fog delay, which allowed coach Bowen Sargent to address his team. He reminded them of the power of no expectations and told them that they could relax, because the pressure was on the other teams and they could just "play golf." They ended up closing the gap by seven shots and secured the tenth spot to advance to the championships.

In 1995, Ben Crenshaw won the Masters. What's remarkable about this achievement is that he arrived at the tournament with his game in shambles, barely making cuts, and the Sunday prior, he had lost his teacher and friend, Harvey Penick. He flew back to Austin for the funeral on Wednesday evening. "I don't know how I got through it," Crenshaw replied. "I still don't." [48]

Probably the most notable display of having no expectations in golf happened during the 2008 Open championship. Padraig Harrington hurt his wrist so badly prior to playing that he only gave himself a 50 percent chance of actually finishing the tournament. In fact, he remarked that if he had not been defending his title, he probably would not have played. "It was a great distraction for me," Harrington said. "It took a lot of pressure off me. It took a lot of stress off me. The fact that I didn't play three practice rounds like normal for a major was a big bonus. I was very fresh going into the weekend, and [these] thirty-six holes was a real battle." [49]

The role of expectations is evident in other sports, too. Jim Breech was an NFL kicker for the Cincinnati Bengals from 1980 to 1992. He holds the Bengals franchise record of 1,152 points and was in route to perhaps becoming the Super Bowl XXIII MVP by scoring ten of the teams sixteen points; however, Joe Montana changed those plans with a "isn't that John Candy" comment to relax his team and a ninety-two-yard culminating touchdown drive. Breech is also a great golfer, and, he discussed his version of having no expectations. Before a road trip to Kansas City, his child jumped on his back, and it immediately seized up. He was still experiencing spasms on the field on Sunday morning and was unsure how he was going to kick at all. Nevertheless, familiar with the fickle world of a professional football, he knew sitting out was not an option, and he would have to perform. He attempted to just keep his back as straight as possible and stay over the ball as he kicked, and although it looked awkward, it was the only way he could kick without pain. Because of his injury, he approached his warm-ups and the game that day completely relaxed with no expectations. He ended up having the best warm-up of his life and was killing the ball during the game. Later on in his career whenever he started struggling, he would remind himself about his "sore back," which would serve as his cue to relax.

The dual roles of golf professional and professional golfer are difficult to navigate. One must maintain appropriate club responsibilities while one attempts to maximize the few chances of actually practicing and playing. This difficulty makes Chip Sullivan's accomplishments on the national level even more spectacular. Sullivan actually achieved all his major accomplishments (1996 Q-school, 2004 PGA Championship finish, and 2008 PGA Professional Championship) while he played with no expectations.

During his 1996 attempt at Q-school finals, he had recently married, and his wife was expecting their first baby. He remarked, "It was the first time in my life that golf was not the most important thing in my life." He finished fourth and secured his PGA Tour card.

During his play in the 2004 PGA Championship, Sullivan finished thirty-first and became the first PGA professional since 1969 to finish under par. His life off the course was even more remarkable. While his wife was expecting their third child (Colby), his sister Kerry was only given a few more days to live because of a fatal liver disease. "I just had to keep my emotions in check and focus on what I was doing," Sullivan said. "I had a lot of emotions flying out there, and I had to stay focused on what I was doing and just play golf." [50]

Perhaps most notable was his win at the 2007 PGA Professional Championship in Sunriver, Oregon, while he was battling health issues. He experienced the effects of a condition called hemochromatosis, which means he retained too much iron in his blood. As a result, he was unable to properly prepare because of his weakened state. Typically, a winner of any national event does not receive twenty-eight pints of blood between January and March.

How could any of these people be expected to perform well? They were able to accomplish greatness in spite of their circumstances because they had no expectations on the outcome. Having no expectations in turn forced them to focus on the aspects within their control. They got out of their own way!

Recall a time in your own game when you were sick, you had outside life issues, you were hurt, or you had a broken or new club, and then note how well you performed. These professional examples and our own testaments are evidence of the power of having no expectations. Having expectations is similar to an invisible ceiling. We know that it's there and how to reach the ceiling. So too, only after we stop focusing on the outcome can we consistently play our best. Expectations do not help us perform better, and they take away from the task at hand. Expectations get in our way.

Tiger Woods often states that he expects to win every tournament; however, he really means that he has the confidence to win every tournament. The difference between confidence and expectations is that expectations are quite simply out of our control, whereas confidence is within our control. The key is confidence in the aspects we can control. We mustn't only pay lip service either. We must believe and perfect the aspects of play that are within our own control.

Practice: No Expectations

"Do something every day for no other reason than you would rather not do it … so that during the hour of dire need, it may find you not unnerved and untrained to stand the test."—*William James*

UCLA head coach Derek Freeman's philosophy of coaching exclusively emphasizes valuing every shot and allowing his players ultimate ownership of their game. Coach Freeman's players are essentially allowed "no excuses" for their play, whether the wind changes directions or a bad bounce happens on a green. During qualifying, he removes the built-in excuses. In doing so, qualifying is made more difficult than actual play.

Coach Freeman sometimes has qualifying rounds by having his team play with irons only. Or if it is a match-play qualifying format, then the "hot" players have to compete without a driver for the round. They are forced to "deal" with being forty to fifty yards behind on most every hole. He sometimes has a rule that the players must miss the green on purpose or that the playing partner gets to drop it in the most difficult spot off the green. Coach Freeman also has UCLA men's golf players qualify by missing the green long or else they get assessed a stroke penalty.

Expectations stem from thinking about the aspects out of our control. How can the UCLA golf team expect to shoot a certain score if they have to contend with missing every green? Coach Freeman removes any expectations before they play and takes any "edge" off of players getting in their own way. These unconventional drills are easily reproducible and help build mental toughness.

Another format that may help people to learn play with no expectations is *playing with someone else's clubs.* Have a difficult putting drill ready, and then try using someone else's putter. If no one else is available, then use an old putter. To strengthen the power of this drill, *play an entire round* with someone else's putter. Take the drill further by switching clubs with a playing partner for the entire round. Chances are that it will not feel correct or comfortable, but it forces you to focus on the aspects you can control and expectations are removed.

Turn off the Light Switch Mentality
"If you don't do it excellently, then don't do it at all."
—John Wooden

Early Sunday morning tee times on the Nationwide Tour are usually devoid of large crowds, and prize money is largely predetermined. [51] While the top fifteen golfers earn 70 percent of the prize monies, the bottom positions split much smaller sums. In fact, there is not much deviation in prize money from fortieth place to sixtieth place on Sunday. Please note that on the Nationwide Tour, the last place finisher will often lose money (due to expenses) after play on the weekend! Add the sometimes drudgery of upcoming travel and next week's tournament preparation, and there is a noticeable difference of enthusiasm levels between early Sunday mornings and Sunday afternoons.

Because of the final day pairings, there is often a *solo* player first to tee off. The running joke is the following: "How fast will he play?" A two-hour round in these circumstances is not uncommon. One season, I was mired in conversation on the practice range with the first player off on Sunday. As we discussed the upcoming day, he replied, "I have played long enough to know when to turn it on and grind it out."

We can bear witness to the player above, notice the veteran experience level, and think, "He's right. It doesn't really matter." However, these are exactly the "light switch" times that can infect one's performance in the future.

The proverbial light switch must always remain "on" during competition, meaning that quitting is not an acceptable option; however, there most likely will be times you want to quit. On the pro tours, it is common for players to withdraw when there is a rain delay that forces a continuance the following day. If a player is out of contention, then waiting around another day to play an "inconsequential" nine holes can be a difficult choice.

In 2006, a British Open qualifier was held in Oakland Hills. For a gauge of difficulty, one only has to look at the scores over par from the 2008 PGA Championship held at the "Monster." The condition of the qualifier was equally difficult, and players were shooting very high scores on the south course. John Senden qualified for his third Open Championship at

Oakland Hills and had remarked that the South Course was brutal and there was no way anyone was shooting under par. Nonetheless, there were several players who started the qualifier poorly and quit.

There is a logical reason why pros would post a DNF; however, quitting is the essence of having a "light switch" mentality. Olin Browne is an example demonstrating why one should never physically quit. During a thirty-six-hole sectional qualifying for the U.S. Open, Browne opened with a seventy-three and actually asked an official about quitting. Deciding against it, however, he proceeded to shoot a fifty-nine, qualify, and led the 2005 U.S. Open after the first round.

Physically withdrawing from play is the most visible sign of a "light switch" mentality, but it is more common with the mental game. A "light switch" mentality is perpetuated by focusing too much on results, and it usually occurs when a player is out of contention or playing poorly. The mentality could become the following: "If I can't win, why compete?" It is normal to respond in these ways, but it serves as a self-presentation measure analogous with kids (or adults) playing a pickup basketball game. After a person plays a one-on-one pickup game and one player jumped out to a seven point lead, the excuses and "smack" soon begin coming out: "I wasn't really trying." "My arms are still tired from working out earlier."

The "light switch" mentality is more than just posting DNF's. It is analogous with complacency or "going through the motions." How one develops this mentality isn't as important as recognizing how to get out of the complacent mindset. Not committing to every shot in practice and competition will eventually lead to a lack of execution in games.

The margin for success is so slim. For the last twenty-five years in major tournaments, the average margin of victory has been less than three strokes! Players must be able to find small ways to maximize their potential. It begins by avoiding a "light switch" mentality and consistently reinforcing quality practice and play.

I have often witnessed players who were seemingly out of the mix with nine holes to go before they proceeded to go on a birdie run. Even though they may only miss the cut by one shot, these moments of play are littered with teachable moments. Players have often told me that it is difficult to recreate feelings of pressure during practice, and I agree. There is a difference between practice and competition. There are also differences between casual rounds, practice rounds, professional amateur tournaments with no substantial outcome, and actual competition. There is also a difference between a Sunday morning tee time and actual contention on Sunday; however, during every round, we can learn something. Did you discover something about your game, develop a carefree attitude or a different focus, or stop caring about the outcome? All rounds can serve as significant moments but only if the "light switch" is turned on.

Practice: Light Switch Mentality
-You'll figure it out.-

Veteran MLB pitchers like Mike Mussina understand the importance of simulating practices as close to games as possible. On one occasion, Mike Mussina was not able to pitch because of severely bad weather. Thus, he warmed up as if he was pitching in a real game by throwing sequences of twenty pitches and sitting down for an "inning." He proceeded to warm back up and to throw the simulated second inning from the stretch. [25]

Quality practice means practicing the way one actually plays. That said, golf practice is usually accomplished through speed and repetition with no breaks, which is counter to real play. To help ensure the "light switch" mentality does not creep in, you must make an effort to simulate the time of actual play during practice.

One strategy of solving the technique problems during practice is to take short breaks (i.e., walking in-between shots). Brief respites allow the mind the necessary break to actually "figure it out." It also provides the opportunity to relax, let go of the built-up frustration, and simulate the real thing. Gestalt therapists have labeled this technique of taking a break "walking around the mountain." The logic is that walking around the mountain and seeing it from all sides allows one the best chance to see the best route up.

Don't Three-Putt
-Winners don't do different things. They do things differently.-

Across putting greens all over the United States, numerous golfers will practice their putting by dropping three balls and putting away. While I have become desensitized to this act, I still ask myself, "Why three balls?" Perhaps the new sleeve of three balls just perpetuates the agreeableness of the number three (three blind mice, the triple play, bad things happen in three's, etc.), and people feel the need to maintain social regularity. Or perhaps most people just fail to prepare properly, and they don't think about what they are actually doing.

The purpose of all practice should be to transfer your skills onto the course, but the three-ball routine has to be one of the worst ways to practice. The last time I checked only one ball is played in competition. Plus, practicing with three balls actually provides a false sense of confidence.

Hypothetically, let's say all three balls stop close to the hole, but what does it actually improve? Because all three balls were putted in about the same spot, the line and speed are already known, thus eliminating two of the major factors in putting. Lastly, most will only rarely remember whether the three balls ended up either short or long. For instance, if someone putts all three balls close to the hole but short, then the player will most likely leave putts short on the course, too.

Everyone practices putting, but how many players approach putting practice with a purpose and a goal? One way to transfer the putting green mentality onto the course is to become creative and competitive with the practice. Create pressure situations by using only *one ball*, emphasizing putting competitions, having goals, and developing and reinforcing feel.

Myth of Multi-practicing
-Have less ... Be more. -

When you are running or working out at the gym, you'll witness most people either listening to music or watching TV. Fitness centers have created environments to promote these practices, adding entire movie theatres for people's cardio sessions. These aforementioned activities are encouraged for beginner's to use these acceptable means of "getting in a workout."

These practices are examples of "disassociation" (distracting the mind with a more pleasant activity). Research has shown that people who employ these techniques are more apt to *adhere* to an exercise program; however, you'll rarely witness a high-caliber marathoner or triathlete listening to music while training. Research has also shown that people who listen to music do not perform as well during strenuous exercise.[52]

Imagine Michael Phelps listening to the newest underwater headphones while swimming. Phelps's training regimen consists of nearly fifty miles of swimming a week, with no outside distractions. Even though these are difficult and grueling practices, his mind rarely wanders to noxious thoughts outside the pool. Though he may sing a song to himself from time to time, his main focus is just touching the wall first. [53]

The way one improves performance is to *associate* (think about the task at hand). Research on effort and cardiovascular tasks reveal that the harder the task, the more people will think about the task at hand. Think about your last strenuous workout or important shot, putt, or dive. Chances are you were not thinking about gardening or watching a movie.

Multitasking is a myth, because while it can be somewhat accomplished, the comprehension, retention, and transfer of learned skills will be severely diminished. We can only focus on one aspect at a time. What is actually occurring is a switching from tasks rapidly: checking e-mail, texting, listening to music, among other tasks. In the present culture, we have succumbed to the banal of technology and believe we are unable to function without these devices.

The sheer amount of information from text messages, e-mails, IMs, and twittering, is staggering. Latest research suggests that "we receive more information in seventy-two hours than our parents received in a month." [54] Today's adolescents and young individuals are exposed to so much technology that they have been dubbed the "digital natives." [55] As a result of the high-tech age, some have coined the new state of mind as "continuous partial attention," in which we partially attend to many tasks as opposed to focusing solely on one. However, the mind is not intended to maintain such partial attention over periods of time, and this prolonged activity can result in impaired cognition. Think about Blackberry's moniker of "crack-berry."

Isn't improving on one's chosen passion the goal of practice? Doing more than one thing at a time usually means doing at least one of them poorly. While low-level tasks like listening to the radio and vacuuming can be performed without complication, the higher-level tasks (e.g., improving one's golf game) require focus.

Golf is a game of interference management that golfers must actually practice maintaining focus. Think for a moment about what distracts and disrupts you during play. Is it the score, maintaining focus, staying committed to the target, course management mistakes, or other players? These interferences occur during most every round, and they are all enacted and thought up in our own mind, which means that we must practice handling these mental workouts.

Practice: Don't Multi-practice
-Focus-

The biggest multitasking culprits for today's golfer are iPods and texting. I am amused by the number of iPods that players take with them to the practice range, and then I'm astonished when golfers are unwilling or unable to give them up. Technology serves great purposes but not when it comes to practicing and multitasking. If one is committed to training and reaching his or her potential, technological distractions must be eliminated from practice and play.

Don't Compare Yourself
"Sometimes, the only way to feel good about yourself is to make others feel bad."
—Homer Simpson

Research suggests that before the age of five, we are focused only on what we can do and are mostly oblivious to the outside world. This stage in development is called the autonomous stage. However, around the age of five, a strange thing occurs. We then become preoccupied with who is fastest and strongest, and we enter a phase of social comparison. [26] Because of the levels of competition through sports, it has remained a part of our thinking ever since we were young. The point is that making comparisons to others is the fastest way to demean our own confidence.

The surest way to feel inadequate, less confident, and unsuccessful is to compare yourself. In order to achieve high self-efficacy, we must rely on our own mental and physical skills, effectively evaluate our own performance, and resist the natural urge to compare ourselves to others as a way to build self-efficacy.

Oddly enough, when we are playing well, we do not make as many comparisons to others; however, there is a natural tendency for social comparison, especially when we are seeking a source of self-confidence. We make more social comparisons when we are not confident and doubt our own abilities. Rarely are we attuned to these events, and more importantly, rarely do these events help. We are not aware of how often we compare ourselves to others, because we have been doing it for so long.

Our frame of reference is limited to recent experiences, so we search for confirmation and confidence from our most recent play. We either compare our current self to the past or other competitors. This becomes evident when we state, "I used to beat such and such easily" or "I used to tear up this course." These types of thoughts and comparisons seem to appear when we are not confident, and we entertain these thoughts because we are understandably searching for confidence. When we are feeling confident, we are more likely to rest in our own decisions and laurels rather than seek outside confirmation by comparing ourselves to others.

Comparing yourself to others or your previous self can even thwart your own game plan during play. For instance, Jim Furyk was one of the most consistent performers in 2006 on tour. He had thirteen top tens and won two events, yet because of Tiger's dominance, he was barely mentioned in the media for his consistent performance.

The presence of Tiger Woods may have caused Furyk to abandon his own game plan on hole seventeen at the 2007 U.S. Open in Oakmont. He was tied for the lead going into the seventeenth with eventual winner Angel Cabera, and he had to make the decision to either drive the short par four (risky play) or lay it up and play to the strengths of his wedge. He decided to drive the green and hit it into the deep rough, but he could not get up and down. Although this is purely speculative, the presence of Tiger Woods following in the final group may have caused him to choose the more risky shot.

Everyone also has a tendency to compare him or her current self to a previous version. We compare a poor outing to a previous great outing, wrongly question ourselves, and experience a lack of self-confidence as a result. The issue isn't necessarily that we make comparisons to our former self, but we undoubtedly become critical of our current self for the wrong reasons instead of looking at issues within our control, mainly our practice or work habits. Comparing ourselves to others or our past self should only be used when we are evaluating our practice habits. In these cases, we hopefully confirm our notion that we are practicing harder and smarter than most everyone else.

The solution is to stop comparing yourself to other people or to your past. Make a commitment to do your best each day, and avoid searching for others as a form of validation.

Keep your mouth off of the ball
-Golf balls don't need landing gear.-

If there's a bad outcome, that does not mean we have to like the outcome, but we do have to accept it. To assess how able someone can accept this outcome involves "talking" to the ball almost immediately after the shot has left the clubface. We all have heard the phrases and even participate from time to time: "Get up." "Down." "Sit." "Get legs." It is not my intention to eliminate all talking to the ball but to bring attention to whether you are a player who always puts your "mouth on the ball" or not. The three or four seconds of "waiting" after the execution of the shot can be worrisome, especially if it was not flush off of the clubface. Nonetheless, most shots in the air do not require assistance from your own mouth and should be left alone.

The execution of the shot is within our control, but no matter how hard we try, the result is not. Often staying in the moment involves the absence of trying to influence the shot and being able to accept where the ball ends up. It also involves being able to let go of past shots and the absence of discussing at length every minute detail of the previous shot.

Mentally Tough Golf Teams

"A rising tide lifts all the boats."
—J.F.K.

Collegiate players have remarked that they play much better golf outside of the team environment. On the other hand, there are players that seem to thrive in the team environment yet shy away from individual tournaments. What are the best ways to bring out the most consistent performances in both types of players?

Prior to the United States winning the 2008 Ryder Cup at Valhalla, Sergio Garcia boasted an amazing 14–4–2 record for Europe. Juxtaposed with Tiger Woods's record of 10-13-2, Sergio's record leads one to think it has more to do with his overall mental processes than his putting stroke. Prior to the 2008 Ryder Cup, Sergio Garcia had previously won fifteen points out of a possible twenty. He was unbeaten in eight foursome matches and stood at 5-1-2 in fourball. His only blemish was that he lost three out of four singles matches in Ryder Cup play.

The 2008 Ryder Cup was his worst performance to date, as he went 0-2-2. His single match play was magnified by his embarrassing 5&4 singles loss to the younger Anthony Kim, which took Sergio's lifetime single record to 1-4. Fairly or unfairly, Sergio's single match play has served as a snapshot of his overall performance during major championships as he faded away after he led at both the (Tiger-less) British Open and PGA Championship.

Sergio Garcia is quite simply the best player who performs even better when in the presence of and part of a team as opposed to playing for himself, and this speaks largely to the differences between team golf and individual golf. It can be explained through the theory of social facilitation. One of the first sport psychology studies examined why some cyclists rode faster when in a group as opposed to cycling by themselves. Researchers later termed the phrase "social facilitation." Well-learned or easy tasks were performed better in the presence of others, whereas difficult tasks were performed worse in the presence of others. [56]

There are two aspects influencing the impact of a team on individual play:

- lack of self-awareness

- level of arousal

First, the lack of self-awareness felt by those who are part of a team may experience a sense of a decreased role, which may facilitate performance. Research by Sorrentino and Sheppard (1978) examined swimmers that either sought out acceptance or avoided rejection. Their research of collegiate swimmers showed that those who sought approval were better swimmers on relay teams and those who avoided rejection swam faster by themselves. [57]

We question why people would destroy their own city by rioting, burning trash cans and cars, or burning couches (e.g., Morgantown, WV) after a home team wins a championship. People in these instances of rioting share a sense of decreased responsibility from the large group and share a loss of self-awareness. [58]

Second, if a player is motivated to seek approval, the role of a team can impact his or her level of arousal during play. Does the presence of a group or team increase or decrease levels of arousal? When these factors combine, it bodes well for players who can blend into part of the team, because they play with a more relaxed attitude. Some team players enjoy their role as a part of a team and can just play. Others feel burdened by their role on a team (usually captains), and they play worse as a result.

Revisiting the 2008 Ryder cup, Sergio Garcia was thrust from merely being a team player to being a central "leader." Sergio now had a "target on his back" by the Americans as a player to beat. Coach Paul Azinger likened Sergio's play to somewhat mystical forces, and he stated prior to the matches, "If you could bottle it, you would probably sell it." This may have been some gamesmanship on behalf of the U.S. coach, but a switch had definitely occurred. Delving a bit further, the 2008 European team was absent of both Darren Clarke and Colin Montgomery, who had been leaders and staples of past victorious teams. Thus, Sergio was thrust into an uncomfortable de facto leadership role. Sergio quite frankly stated "I'm not going to kick out my chest and say I'm the leader of this team, no" [59]

Also, even though Sergio Garcia was unbeaten in nine foursome matches, coach Nick Faldo benched him during the Saturday morning foursome pairings. His rationale was to give both Sergio Garcia and Lee Westwood, who had both played in twenty-two straight matches, a rest before the afternoon. Lee Westwood stated his frustration when he said, "I wanted to play … This is the Ryder Cup. I would play with my arm hanging off."[60] While it may have worked in terms of the morning matches (Europe won two), it didn't seem to help the mentality of Sergio Garcia.

Obviously, the cause of Sergio playing better as a member of a team is open to debate, but there are different factors to consider. Benching a captain sometimes may work, but it is a calculated move and one in which the coach should know how the player will respond. Also, the role of not having to post a score in a team environment may allow players to avoid being scrutinized and play with a more relaxed demeanor.

Coaches often stress the importance of building a strong cohesive team, but the cohesion is almost always directed toward a common goal like winning a championship or tournament. When coaches stress an emphasis on achieving a goal, it is called task cohesion; however, in co-acting sports, like golf and baseball, everyone operates separate from each other, and task cohesion often can be a detriment to performance. Players can become focused on "carrying" the team and trying harder, and they inevitably play worse.

Practice: Team Golf
"Those who smile go the extra mile."
—Anonymous

As a means of building a strong team, one should focus on creating social cohesion, also known as team chemistry. The analogy of a team as a family is often very accurate. Everyone does not get along all the time, but the sense of belonging still remains. Strong teams often operate as a family, and creating this environment depends on two main components: assuming roles and bonding as a team.

First, as within a family, there are roles that each member should accept. Effectively communicating and knowing appropriate roles can prevent unrest and discouragement later. For example, a team's number one and two players may have different roles entering tournaments than players ranked four or five may have. Joe Skovron, former coach of the golf team at the University of Laverne, is adamant that his players assumed "specific roles." Because he has played the mini-tours and caddied for Rickie Fowler on the PGA Tour, he knows the small difference between finishing in the top thirty or the top ten is usually due in part to course management. "I often have to tell my number five player that we don't need a sixty-seven from him. We need center of the green," stated Skovron.

Also, qualifying for collegiate tournaments often arises as events that can make accepting roles difficult. If a player has played summer amateur events and has finished well, should that person still be required to qualify? If a player finishes in the top five of a tournament, should he or she have to return that week to qualify? Regardless of the coach's policy, it helps if this information is clearly communicated.

Players can accept their roles if they first know the opportunities and feel appreciated for both effort and ability. Bray and colleagues (2005) discovered that players whose roles were clear were more satisfied than players whose roles were ambiguous. [61] In turn, athletes who were more satisfied displayed more persistence and effort in competition. To help clarify roles, players want to know the answers to the following questions:

- *How will play be determined?*

- *What do I need to improve upon?*

- *How will my performance be evaluated?*

- *What are the consequences?*

As players assume their roles it impacts team chemistry. Take some time to recognize your team. While it is ultimately you who must execute, there are others on the team who can help you reach your goal. Having a mentally tough team means to support, congratulate, encourage, confide in, or thank them. The following is a three-step process for building team chemistry: (1) care, (2) prepare, and (3) share.

(1) *Care about your team:* Have a genuine interest in the other person. This goes beyond the course and translates into personal lives. In short, teammates should know that people care about them. A few questions to answer regarding your team:

- *Whom do you most appreciate on the team?*

- *What are his or her main strengths, and have you told them lately?*

- *Who can you improve your relationship with on the team?*

- *What can you do to improve this relationship?*

(2) *Prepare like a team:* One way to assess how well everyone is preparing is for each player to recognize the hardest worker. Teams have enlisted awards, such as a box of nails (toughness) or tub of glue (togetherness), to recognize certain achievements as well. For instance, the "lunch pail" is Virginia Tech's football symbol, which is given to the defensive player who performs best in a game or practice since the tragic massacre on campus, it has even assumed a symbol of team and university unity as well (visit the site at hokiesports.com). Preparing as a team also transfers into competition. Knowing that teammates have undergone the same tough demands and sacrifices in practice connects a team so that each puts forth the best effort in competition even during tough stretches.

(3) *Share as a team:* Develop team cohesion outside of golf. This can be achieved by spending time with one another through simple activities like a weekly basketball game, a movie, a card game, or a "Playstation" night. Everyone should be a part of the activity. Former head coach of the University of Tennessee's baseball team, Rod Delmonico, summarized sharing as a team quite easily when he said, "We try to do a lot of things together as a team. We'll attend football games as a group. We play basketball together and have team meals together both at home and on the road. In essence, we try to get the players to know each other not just as baseball players but as students and human beings." The gatherings need not necessarily concern hanging out; it can be used as a means for players to check-in with one another. Luke Hocheaver, the number one draft pick in 2006 MLB draft, conducted "senior sessions" at Tennessee. The seniors

would meet separate from the team and call out one another for dogging it in practice or recognize each other for how hard they had been working.

Team Penalty
"I need you to stay confident. You're doing fine, but I need you."
—Gary Christian

I had made an atrocious error while I was caddying for the affable Brit, Gary Christian, at the 2006 Knoxville Open. It was the second day on the ninth hole of the Nationwide Tour event. He tossed me the ball after he stuck his approach on the par five to about fifteen feet. Because I had recently graduated with my doctorate from the University of Tennessee, the crowd was favoring the local, to say the least, and I briefly lost my own concentration in the moment. As he tossed me the ball, it fell into the bag, and I reached in and retrieved; however, this ball was a Callaway 4 logo with a blue circle instead of the Callaway 2 like the one he had just tossed me. As Gary made the breaking putt, my heart sank, because it was then that I realized I had made a mistake. He had just birdied the hole to go six under and capture some momentum. I told him of my gaffe as he headed to the next tee.

According to rule 15-2 (substituted ball), he would incur a penalty of two strokes after he declared the penalty on himself. Through no fault of his own, he started the back nine at four under par, and within a sport where every stroke really does count, this was potentially devastating. My own "voice" started in on me with unrelenting hatred—and most deservedly. "You just cost your golfer two strokes. Great work. You don't even deserve to be out here right now. I can't believe you did that!"

The most troubling aspect of this situation was that I had just hurt my teammate, and this was the major cause of my feelings of worthlessness mentioned above. Spoiling my teammate's chances hurt even worse. While this story has many different lessons with regard to mental toughness, (e.g., staying in the present, bouncing back, "the voice") the purpose of this anecdote is to emphasize the importance of the team.

Gary remained mostly silent for two holes, birding hole ten, but he later approached me after the next hole, noticing my body language and the major shift in my mood. He looked me in the eye and said, "I need you to stay confident here. You're doing fine, but I need you." *Bam!* Just like that, all of my negative muttering disappeared, and it was replaced with a renewed determination and focus on the task at hand, namely helping my teammate. His simple words of encouragement and support were tremendous, and it encompassed the power of belief in the concept of team. Don't underestimate the power of your words as well. By the way, Gary Christian finished alone in second in that event by more than four shots.

The Net-Generation Gap
"Flattery is like perfume. It's fine to smell. Just don't drink it."
—Coach Brad Stevens

The way to build mental toughness is for young golfers to fail and learn how to best handle failure. At a mini-tour event a few years ago, a young amateur (with trust fund money) was entered, and his mother was present. She struck up a long conversation about her son and mentioned that his swing coach (top ten in the country) had eliminated his high scores. She stated, "I am glad he won't shoot any high seventies anymore." All I thought was the following, "Wow, what happens when he does?"

The fragile mentality of young golfers is becoming especially apparent today. Stuart Appleby noted as much in an interview with *Golf Digest*. He stated, "In Australia, if you're a promising athlete, you never, ever hear, 'We'll get you whatever you want.' Or 'Anything we can do for you?' Over here [U.S.], young hotshot athletes are promoted early and can get caught up in it." [62]

Parents' vast investment in their children perpetuates an economic force behind young golfers to succeed. Golfers are required to specialize too early and withdraw from other sports as a means to become a better golfer. More often than not, the opposite occurs. They are placed under undue pressure and burn out from the sport more quickly. Consequently, youth can lack the perspective, motor development, and "toughness" that other sports can provide. Jon Stutz, Head professional at Purgatory Golf Club seemed to put it in perspective when he questioned, "How many current NBA players were only in structured leagues growing up? They were on the playground fending for themselves." Remember that Earl Woods was the one who had Tiger playing other sports. He left it up to a young Tiger to choose which sport he wanted to play.

Golfers can develop their picturesque swing on the range while they repeat the same lie and yardage every time. What becomes lost is the art of actually playing golf: cultivating creativity on the greens, managing emotions, course management, interacting with others, and most importantly, fostering perseverance.

There always appears to be a similar mentality when different generations refer to each other. Comments such as "this generation just doesn't get it" or "kids today" display an aura of authority; however, when it comes to the current generation of Millennials and Echo-Boomers (birthdates 80s and 90s), the perceived overconfidence is well-founded. As coaches, teachers, and players, we must understand and appreciate the current generation. Because of technological advances and our reliance on digital information, members of the new generation are indeed the experts of today in many ways.

Millennials express themselves through social networks like Facebook, MySpace, Twitter, and YouTube sites. They use laptops, buy cell phones, download ringtones, play interactive video games, and watch reality television.[63] Speed and innovativeness are also cherished. Instant (not just quick) feedback is expected, and the best products and gadgets are desired for the newest improvements over past models.

Because of their individual nature, Millennials *expect* creative coaching, and they *expect* to be empowered to make decisions, too. They want rules for their participation as part of a collaborative group, but they also still desire an ability to "shine." These norms create challenges in order to simultaneously connect to and challenge the current generation.

The social norms of the current generation have drifted so dramatically toward instant gratification and positive feedback that youths (and parents) often seem to have lost sight of the "big picture." The expectation of immediately achieving and obtaining anything a person wants ultimately transfers into sports. There is also a new mentality of "entitlement" that says, "If I don't get what I want, then it's not me. It's you."

At some point, sports become the great equalizer, because the score does not lie. We either win or lose. We execute the shot, or we don't. We make the putt or miss it, and no amount of negotiating or complaining can change the results. Though defeat and setbacks occur in sport and life, the only way to overcome these hardships is to build effective coping strategies.

Finish Strong

"Scientists have proven that it's impossible to long-jump thirty feet, but I don't listen to that kind of talk. Thoughts like that have a way of sinking into your feet."
—Carl Lewis

Evaluating Performance

Redelmeier and Kahneman (1996) discovered that colonoscopy patients differed in their overall experiences. One group had a standard colonoscopy, while the second group had a colonoscopy "plus." The "plus" was an additional minute with the instrument still in place with no additional movement. Thus, although the overall unpleasantness was actually longer in duration, the "plus" group of patients actually judged their experience as less unpleasant because of the mild pain at the end of the procedure. Five years after the exam, the patients in the "plus" group were more likely to comply with requests for follow-up exams than the standard patients. The results suggest that their experience was dictated more by the ending than the overall procedure. [64]

The more often we are able to finish strong, the more often our score will reflect our actual performance. Perhaps more importantly, finishing strong engrains good thoughts into our memory. Additional research has found that our memories are most affected by the ways events end, including positive experiences, later dubbed the Peak-End rule. [65]

Finishing strong is applicable within golf, too. Think about the hypothetical scenario of bogeying holes thirteen and fourteen, yet finishing by birding holes seventeen and eighteen. We would rarely reflect on our play as "poor," because our latest memories are good thoughts and scores. However, let's reverse the scenario and say we birdie holes thirteen and fourteen and bogey holes seventeen and eighteen. The score is exactly the same (all things considered), yet finishing poorly may have more of an impact than the score. Because "we are our memories" and we lack the capability to unconsciously recall all shots, we are reduced to evaluating and remembering the last holes of our play.

If we finish poorly, the bitter emotions leave us with a reduced sense of accomplishment. In turn, our confidence may become diminished, because when we try to recall our play, we immediately think of the last holes. If this cycle repeats itself enough, then we become relegated to irrational thoughts and beliefs: "I can't finish" or "When is the bad hole coming?" Unfortunately, the repetition of any types of thoughts (positive or negative) turns into a self-fulfilling prophecy. If we expect good things or expect bad things to happen, then it turns into a reality. In summation, it is greatly important that we finish strong, no matter how we are doing.

Practice: Finish Strong
"How Are Your 52s?"
—Coach John Reis

Coach John Reis from the University of Cincinnati had his players evaluate their play on *how well they finished*. He contested that if players can finish strong, then it is likely that they will have played well. He stated that the finishing holes are the times that players switch either their game plan or their mentality by thinking too much about the score. Players may become overly cautious or more aggressive in either sense. Thus, it becomes a mental challenge to block out thoughts of the score and focus on the upcoming hole.

As a result, evaluating performance this way combines many factors: overall score, handling pressure, and consistency. Lastly, the better the memories, the more improved confidence individuals will have for future performances. Reis labeled this system "how are your 52s?" Evaluate your performance on how well you finish using the simple formula of: (8 + 9) + (17 + 18) = 52. If we are consistently over par on our 52s, then we must make more of an effort to finish strong.

Golf is like Railroad Tracks
-Any long jump takes a running start.-

Golf is like railroad tracks because there are two sides. We will always like a part of our game and dislike the other(s). We could have driven the ball great, struck our irons well, but we just did not make any putts. On one side, we could have played badly, but actually made some putts and managed to post a good score. The game is similar to railroad tracks.

If we are not playing consistent, then we are not accomplishing one of the following:

- We are not practicing enough,

- We are not working on the correct things,

- We are putting too much pressure on ourselves.

These keys to success are not easy, but they are necessary to playing consistent golf. Hopefully, this book has helped you take a step toward building mental toughness.

References

1. Krampe, R., & Ericsson, K. (1996). Maintaining excellence: Deliberate practice and elite performance and young and older pianists. *Journal of Experimental Psychology, 125*, 331–-359.

2. Ericsson, K. (2001). The path to expert golf performance: Insights from the masters on how to improve performance by deliberate practice. In P. R. Thomas (Ed.), *Optimizing performance in golf* (pp. 1-57). Brisbane, Australia: Australian Academic Press.

3. Frankl, V. (1959). *Man's search for meaning*: Simon & Schuster, New York.

4. Sackett, D., & Torrance, G. (1978). The utility of different health states as perceived by the general public. *Journal of Chronic Diseases, 31*, 698–704.

5. Gilbert, D. (2006). *Stumbling on happiness*. New York: Random House.

6. Batterson, M. (2006). *In a pit with a lion on a snowy day*. New York: Water Brook Multnomah.

7. Machowicz, R. (2008). *Unleash the warrior within*. Cambridge: Da Capo Press.

8. Cleveland, M. (1999). *Dover solo. New York:* MMJ press.

9. Golf.com (May 15, 2007). Friend of Tiger, Phil battles brain tumor. Retrieved on September 2007 from http://www.golf.com/golf/tours_news/article/0,28136,1621257,00.html.

10. Strohmeyer, D. (June, 1 2009). Tom Brady is back, *Sports Illustrated*, 110, 22, p. 34.

11. Bull, S., Albinson, J., & Shambrook, C. (1996). *The mental game plan: Getting psyched for sport.* WV: Fitness Information Technology.

12. Stone, O. (producer and director). (1999). *Any Given Sunday* [motion picture] United States: Warner Bros. Pictures.

13. Stapleton, A. (July, 24, 2004). Franco back on top in Milwaukee, *Park City Daily News*, 4B.

14. PGA Tour. (2009). *What they said: Anthony Kim.* Retrieved Nov 23, 2009 from PGATour.com: http://www.pgatour.com/2009/tournaments/r016/01/06/tuesday_transcript_kim/index.html.

15. Langer E. & Rodin J. (1976). The effects of choice and enhanced personal responsibility for the aged: a field experiment in an institutional setting. *Journal of Personality and Social Psychology.* 34, 191-198.

16. Hogan, B. (1957). *Five lessons: The modern fundamentals of golf.* New York: Simon & Schuster.

17. Beilock, S., Carr, T., MacMahon, C., & Starkes, J. (2002). When paying attention becomes counterproductive: Impact of divided versus skill-focused attention on novice and experienced performance of sensorimotor skills. *Journal of Experimental Psychology, 8*, 6-16.

18. Dusek, D. (October, 2005). *The new way to putt.* Golf Magazine, 95-97.

19. Orton, K. (2004, August 10th). After 24, 801 miles, she's a woman on the run. *Washington Post*.

20. Stevens, J. (1988). Marathon monks of Mount Hiei. Boston, MA Shambhala.

21. Hack, D. (September, 21, 2006). Lehman's Difficult Rise Stirs U.S. Ryder Cup Team *New York Times*, Sports section.

22. Nelson, C. (December 5, 2007). The PGA Tour's Q-School is arguably the most intense competition in sports. *The Occidental Weekly*.

23. Armchairgolfblog. (January 16, 2006). *No regrets for Colt Knost.* Retrieved July 17 2007 from: http://armchairgolfblog.blogspot.com/2008/01/no-regrets-for-colt-knost.html.

24. Michaelis, V. (June 2, 2008). Judo's former prodigy marshals her life, talents, *USA Today*.

25. Feinstein, J. (2008). *Living on the black*. New York: Little Brown & Co.

26. Weinberg, R., & Gould, D. (2006). *Foundations of sport and exercise psychology (4th edition)*. Champaign, IL: Human Kinetics.

27. Kahneman, D., & A. Tversky. (1979). Prospect theory: An analysis of decision under risk. *Econometrica 47*, 263–291.

28. O'Connor, I. (2008). *Arnie & Jack: Palmer, Nicklaus, and golf's greatest rivalry*. New York: Houghton Mifflin Co.

29. Bandura, A. (1997). *Self-efficacy: The exercise of control*. New York: Worth Publishers.

30. Shipnuck, A. (June 9, 2008). Simply the best. *Sports Illustrated* 108, 23, 68–-75.

31. Vealey, R., & Greenleaf, C. (2006). Seeing is believing: Understanding and using imagery in sport. In J. M. Williams (Ed.), *Applied sport psychology: Personal growth to peak performance* 5th ed. (pp. 285-305). Mountain View, CA: Mayfield Publishing.

32. Fletcher, D. (2006). British swimming, sports psychology, and Olympic Medals: Is it all in the mind?!? *World Swimming Coaches Association Newsletter* 6, 2: 8.

33. Campbell, S. (April 12th, 2009). Epps lends Cabrera a helping hand. *Houston Chronicle*, Sports.

34. Bray, M. (1998). Self-modeling as an intervention for stuttering. *School Psychology Review* 27, 587-598.

35. Singh: How to practice, if not play, like the world's no.1 golfer. (2005). *The Washington Post*, Sports.

36. Colt's president Polian opens up about team's ride to the AFC title game. (2007, January 18). *USA Today*, Sports.

37. Simpson, J. (2004). *Touching the void*. New York: Perennial.

38. Fendrich, H. (September, 12, 2006). Almost Grand. *Ocala-Star Banner, 6D*.

39. Jenkins, S. & Armstrong, L. (2000). *It's not about the bike*. New York: Penguin Putnam.

40. Aesop (1909). *Fox and the sour grapes*. The Harvard Classics, New York: P.F. Collier & Son, 17.

41. Pavlovich, L. (2004). Navy SEAL Training: How USA Gold Medal Softball Team Utilized Rugged Mental Conditioning, *Collegiate Baseball*, 45, 14.

42. Van Sickle, G. (2008, Nov 17th). Last ditch. *Sports Illustrated*, vol. 109, 19 G6–G10.

43. Bell, R., Cox, K., & Finch, W. (2009). Pre-putting routines and success of collegiate golfers. *Journal of Sport Behavior.*

44. Beilock, S., Bertenthal, B., McCoy, A., & Carr, T. (2004). Haste does not always make waste: Expertise, direction of attention, and speed versus accuracy in performing sensorimotor skills. *Psychonomic Bulletin & Review, 11,* 373-379.

45. Kingston, K. & Hardy, L. (2001) Pre-performance routine training using holistic process goals. In P.R. Thomas (Ed.), *Optimising Performance in Golf* (pp. 264-278). Brisbane, Australia: Australian Academic Press.

46. Brown, C. (August 18, 2000). Golf; Woods with no sign of weakness, shares lead. *New York Times*, Sports.

47. PGA Tour (n.d). K.J. Choi Media Guide. Retrieved September 9, 2008, from the PGA Tour website: http://www.pgatour.com/players/02/43/57/media-guide.html.

48. Richards, P. (June, 25, 2009). Crenshaw eager to end drought. *The Indianapolis Star,* B10.

49. Ferguson, D. (July 20, 2008). Harrington wins British Open. *The Boston Globe*, Sports.

50. Pump, B. (2004). Sullivan lowest club professional at PGA since 1969. Retrieved from:http://www.pga.com/pgachampionship/2004/news_081504_sullivan_lowest_club.html.

51. Brown, J. (2009) Quitter's never win: The (Adverse) incentive effects of competing with superstars. *Journal of Political Economy.*

52. Tenenbaum, G., & Ecklund, R. (Eds.). (2007). *Handbook of Sport Psychology.* New Jersey: Wiley & Sons.

53. Michaelis, V. (August 1, 2008). Built to swim, *USA Today*, 1A–2A.

54. Geraci, R. (January, 2008). *Don't be overwhelmed by technology,* Reader's Digest, 106–110.

55. Small, G., & Vorgan, G. (2008). *iBrain: Surviving the technological alteration of the modern mind.* New York: Harper Collins.

56. Zajonc, R., Heingartner, A., & Herman, E. (1969). Social enhancement and impairment of performance in the cockroach. *Journal of Personality and Social Psychology, 13,* 83–92.

57. Sorrentino, R., & Sheppard, B. (1978). Effects of affiliation-related motives on swimmers in individual versus group competition: A field experiment. *Journal of Personality and Social Psychology, 36,* 704–714.

58. Tesser, A. (1995). *Advanced Social Psychology.* New York: McGraw-Hill.

59. Elbin, K. (September, 16, 2008). An Interview with: Sergio Garcia and Soren Hansen. Retrieved from The Ryder Cup website: http://www.rydercup.com/2008/news/2008/europe/09/16/garcia_hansen_091608/index.html.

60. Newberry, P. (September, 9, 2008). Europeans make their move at Ryder Cup. *USA Today*, Sports.

61. Bray, S., Beauchamp, M., Eys, M., & Carron, A. (2005). Does the need for role clarity moderate the relationship between role ambiguity and athlete satisfaction? *Journal of Applied Sport Psychology, 17,* 306–318.

62. Verdi, B. (September, 2007). Stuart Appleby: The Golf Digest Interview. *Golf Digest Magazine.*

63. Tapscott, D. (2008). Grown up Digital: How the Net Generation is Changing Your World. Mc-Graw-Hill.

64. Kahneman, D., Fredrickson, B., Schreiber, C., & Redelmeier, D. (1993). When more pain is preferred to less: Adding a better end. *Psychological Science,* 4, 401–405.

65. Redelmeier, D., & Kahneman, D. (1996). Patients' memories of painful medical treatments: Real-time and retrospective evaluations of two minimally invasive procedures. *Pain, 66,* 3–8.

LaVergne, TN USA
23 June 2010
187172LV00005B/8/P

9 781449 061883